SHINE ON YOU CRAZY DAISY
- VOLUME 6

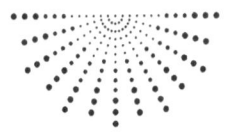

COMPILED BY TRUDY SIMMONS

CONTENTS

Acknowledgments	vii
Introduction	ix
1. Work In Progress	1
2. With Love Through Loss to Global Movement	7
3. Find Your Path and Listen To Your Soul	14
4. Lickety Split	21
5. After it Falls apart	27
6. Behind the Mask	34
7. The Weirdo in the Room	41
8. It's Time to Play	48
9. Can You Change the world	54
10. Glass Houses	61
11. My Musical Heart	68
12. Being Alive. It's Everything.	75
13. Fall down seven, get up eight Lady!	82
14. Navigating through life's storms	89
15. So, what now...?	96
16. Shining the Light Within	102
17. Horse Wisdom for Women	109
18. 3 things I've learnt in my first year as a Mompreneur	117
19. Is Your Life Aligned with Your Values?	124
20. From Sales to Sex Therapist	130
21. The Final Bow	137
22. Having it all	143
23. Want to Know the 3 Keys to Happiness, Satisfaction and Success?	149
24. Do It Before You're Ready!	157
25. My Journey to Today	165
26. A Rising Mind, Like a Rising Tide, Lifts All Boats	172

About The Daisy Chain Group   181
Every time you buy from a small business, they do a happy dance!   183
Other books   185

Volume Editor's Part of the Work © Trudy Simmons
Each Chapter © of the Contributor
All rights reserved

This book or any portion thereof may not be reproduced or used in any manner whatsoever without the express written permission of the relevant copyright holders except for the use of brief quotations in a book review.

Trudy Simmons and The Daisy Chain Group International Ltd do not have any control over, or responsibility for, any third-party websites referred to or in this book. All internet addresses were correct at the time of publication. Should these addresses change, we regret any inconvenience caused, but cannot accept responsibility for such changes.

Printed in the United Kingdom
First Printing, September 2022

ISBN: 9781739743109 (paperback)
ISBN: 9781739743116 (eBook)

The Daisy Chain Group International Ltd
Hampshire, UK
connect@thedaisychaingroup.com

This book is dedicated to....
....All the businesswomen that are showing up and putting themselves out there to be seen and heard. We are all in this together... this is for you to take inspiration, that we are all on a similar journey, but taking different paths, with varying bumps along the way to here.
You can do it! Keep going!
Shine Bright and Shine On.

ACKNOWLEDGMENTS

This is to acknowledge and appreciate all of those that have contributed and shared a piece of their journey with us all in this book. Thank you for your courage and tenacity. You are all inspirational.

This is the 6th volume in the series and has allowed me to share the stories of 168 businesswomen through the books and the Shine On You Crazy Daisy podcast within a YEAR! The first book was launched on the 7th September 2021 and the 6th book is launching on the 7th September 2022. I am very proud of the whole project.

Here is to the lessons we didn't want to learn; that we didn't know we had to learn to get us to where we are now. Be grateful for the good AND the bad.

Each of these brilliant businesswomen have shared a part of their journey and each of us knows that we can't do it alone, we aren't meant to do it alone. Surround yourself with the people that "get it".

To the Facebook communities that I run – Businesswomen Shine Online and Hampshire Women's Business Group for showing me each and every day that whatever we are going through, we are all there for each other. For being the communities that we all call "our lounge-room" where we come to share, ask for help, support, advice and give from our expertise without expectations. I am grateful for the "tribe" that we have and that like attracts like. Community is everything on this lonely road. Come and join ours, it is the best – tee hee!

I stand for inclusion on all aspects. The baseline of everything that we build is on kindness and being available with open arms to all businesswomen that wish to be a part of something and want to be seen and heard. We are here for all of that.

Welcome.

INTRODUCTION

This book is about creating a platform for businesswomen to have an inspirational voice and to share their stories with others, to show that this entrepreneurial rollercoaster is the highs AND the lows and that we navigate them all differently, but hopefully with a tribe/team of people that support our vision to our success – whatever that looks like, and it is different for everyone.

Each story is unique, each story is REAL, each story offers a piece of insight, motivation and encouragement when we need it the most. You are not alone.

These are un-edited chapters of real stories from women that have been where you are and have stories to share about how to find your way, not feel isolated, find out what you CAN do, rather than feeling stuck in what you think you can't do.

These…. Are their stories!! Bong bong…

Charity donation

As we gain, so can we give – that is my philosophy of running my own business. 10% of the profits from this book will be donated to the bereaved families of the NHS who have died while looking after us and our families during the Corona-Virus pandemic.

To find out more, or to donate, please visit this website – www.healthcareworkersfoundation.org

1
WORK IN PROGRESS

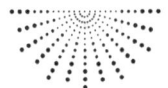

Trudy Simmons

I love it when I get bored; it becomes a feeling of utter desire to DO SOMETHING and do something different, or differently.

There've been so many times when this feeling takes over and I shake things up – in my life, in my business, in my relationships. To me, being bored is the most uncomfortable feeling; it is a visceral feeling that makes me feel like I have ants in my pants and bats in my belfry – I can't sit still!

And this is that weird feeling between, "oh Trudy, relax and take time off" and "I'm so bored I need to DO something, anything…EVERYTHING".

When I get bored in business, it can help me come up with the next big idea, or the next way to engage and communicate with people. When I get bored in life, it can make me pack everything up into a suitcase and move countries, take off for a couple of months, or sell my house.

I'm a doer. It is part of my DNA: I simply can't talk about doing something "one day", or "I wish" – I get it done. And ordinarily, I don't let anything get in my way – no matter how illogical or unpractical that may seem to some people. I need to be able to DREAM. I need to be able to have space to THINK BIG and then create. Just let me dream...

This is the thing with creative people and businesswomen, we need to be able to dream, we need to be able to share our crazy ideas and for that one person to say – GO FOR IT – rather than putting all the "things" in the way. It is so easy for us to listen and hear the nay-sayers and squash our little sparkles of ideas that could be the next big thing. You just never know – and you just never know, because sometimes, when we listen to others, we don't dip our toe in the water, let alone take the giant leap off the cliff that it sometimes takes to feel like we are going in OUR direction.

So, back to being bored and angry. When I'm bored, I feel angry because I don't know what to do. I feel angry because I'm frustrated that I'm not doing all the things at the same time, and I feel angry because I feel like I'm failing at the things that I am good at – while also failing because I'm not doing the things that I'm bad at either!

And what do I do at this point (besides making sure to stomp my feet un-necessarily loudly and walk around heavy sighing until someone asks what is wrong!)? I find a way to get unstuck.

We get STUCK in boredom and anger – we feel stuck, and we don't know what to do to fix it. Sometimes, this stuck-edness is because something, anything, EVERYTHING needs to change, and that can feel just as uncomfortable as boredom!

I've been here; I go to this place regularly; I stay here; I move from here, and I don't look back.

I have been told that I have an "abnormal ability" – WAIT that wasn't the end of the sentence – "I have an abnormal ability to let go of things very easily". As I've gained age and (*ahem*) wisdom, I know this to be true. I've been through and continue to face all kinds of trauma; big life changing trauma, little daily trauma, prolonged trauma that reaches far down into the depths of my battered soul and wreaks havoc on my ability to function. BUT... when I feel that it is finished, I'm done – I let it go, and I move on. Not because I can, but because I must – pain doesn't help me to be what I want to be. Pain and trauma don't allow me to be there for my business communities, for my networking groups, for my business.

So, like an annoying buzzy-fly... I look over my shoulder and it is gone.

Doing what I could until I could let go

Why on earth is this a part of my Crazy Daisy story? Because all of us, whether we have an "abnormal ability" to let go or not, get stuck sometimes.

My mission in my business is to show up, turn up, be bold, be brave, be visible and to entertain businesswomen with various platforms that allow them to be seen and heard. It is really hard to turn up, let alone show up and be visible when you are stuck in the past, stuck in the trauma, stuck in the anger, stuck in being and feeling bored.

We have so much to offer, so much to do, so many people that we want to be able to help, the list is endless. But that list will feel like a noose around your neck IF you can't find the energy to be there for yourself and by extension, your business and, as an extra extension to that, your audience.

For us to be able to show up in and for our businesses, we have to be prepared for the tough times. We get prepared by learning from others who have been there before us.

Over this last year, I have been stuck in a trauma response, having to react to each day as it comes, needing to be very careful about how I showed up, where my energy was spent, how I was able to support other people and how I was best able to do what I HAD to do – I didn't have it in me to do any more than was necessary – and that was ok.

I didn't bash myself upside the head or do daily-virtual-self-flagellation because I couldn't do more than I was doing. I stayed with it. I got up each day with the dream of what it would feel like when this "bit" was over and normal life could resume.

For me, what I could do was turn up to the things that were already planned, in the diary, scheduled. I LOVED turning up, pressing "START" and seeing the people in the online networking events, meeting new clients, getting out of my head and into theirs. My absolute joy is making people laugh, and as my Grandma says, "laughter is the best medicine"; for those moments, those sessions, those people, I was so, so grateful. I would turn up not knowing if I would burst into tears or shut everything down, and I would leave with that little heartbeat that kept saying "you're doing it, you're doing it, you're doing it".

I couldn't just let go of this trauma and be "normal". Why? Because you can't let go of something when you're in the thick of it. And for me, I couldn't talk about it when I was in it. I had people in my community ask if I was ok because I wasn't as visible, because I wasn't available, because I didn't get back to people in a nano-second.

In these times, there was no "I'm bored" or "I'm angry" – I was just surviving. And I know that you get that. We have all been in these phases of life, where we are just getting by.

These are not the times to try to take more on, to grow the list, to expand anything. Feeling expansive didn't feel possible at all. Everything felt like walking through sticky treacle with a 1000 pound weight around my ankle and each step forward took effort – and some days, that effort was too much.

Luckily for me, there was a date and a conclusion for my "surviving-chapter" – and when that day came, I sat with it. I spent the next few days processing it, and then…. I was done. That's not to say that my body doesn't need time to catch up – I'm tired. But my mind is free and buzzing and ready and open and wanting to dream again!

My mind has that door open to a space of creativity that was shut for months.

I'm sharing, possibly oversharing. I'm letting you know that if you're stuck in something, stuck in a mindset, stuck in a story, stuck in a phase of your life, look at the ways in which you need to let go. What needs to happen so that you can move on? What can change so that you can DREAM? You are not alone in this part of your story.

Unstuck and ready for action

So now, I'm bored – not in a "nothing matters" way, but in an "ohhhhh what's next" way. In a "dream big, come up with something, plan it, do it" way. My mind is abuzz with white noise, and I just need to find space and time (pfft, I hear you saying! Space and time – what's that??) to sit and listen to what is behind that white noise. I need an anchor to give this Crazy Daisy the ability to go "that's it; that's the one; let's go!"

I feel like I've been a daisy at dusk for the past year – closing its petals for protection. I've felt like a genie in a bottle without a voice or a way of going POOFT – I am here, and it is MAGICAL.

Now, change is in the air! Look out, and brace yourselves – something is coming, something is changing, and it feels like the future is around the corner. I'm poking my head around there and going "ohhhh THERE YOU ARE, I'm ready. Bring it on!"

BIO:

Trudy Simmons is a Clarity and Productivity Business Coach for women entrepreneurs. She has a truckload of empathy and a little bit of hard-arse!

She helps you find out WHAT you want to do, WHY you want to do it, and HOW to get it DONE!

She loves to show her audience how to become more successful by getting clarity, taking action, and following through. Trudy has 20 years' experience in helping people move from being stuck and not knowing the next step, to getting their shizzle DONE by finding and harnessing their strengths and removing their weaknesses!

She knows what keeps you up at night – the thousand ideas that are germinating in your brain – and she knows how to sort them into "no go", "maybe later", and "hells yes", and get done what's really important to your success.

She's the creator and founder of the Shine On You Crazy Daisy membership – which gives you the opportunity to grow your tribe, expand your audience, take in monthly knowledge – Online Networking is the quickest and smartest way to grow your business! The membership also offers a VIP option to be able to work ON your business in online co-working and focus and accountability fortnightly group coaching.

www.thedaisychaingroup.com

2
WITH LOVE THROUGH LOSS TO GLOBAL MOVEMENT

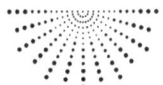

Marie Alessi

Rob was supposed to wake me at 7.30am. I woke up at 7.31. Something felt different.
I could *always* rely on my husband. I didn't hear from him all morning and all my text messages and attempted phone calls remained unanswered. At lunch time I had the nudge to call the hotel he was staying at whilst on a business trip in Western Australia.

I asked them to check his room, as I was worried about him.

Four excruciating hours later my phone rang, a number from WA. "I am sorry to inform you that your husband deceased in a hotel room in Perth this morning." My world stopped. It felt like a needle scratching over the record while playing our favourite happy song. Everything drowned in silence, my heart echoing in my chest. Simply surreal.

Our boys were sitting downstairs in the living room, dressed for their Hapkido training, waiting for me to make "just one more phone call". As I stepped downstairs my brain was trying to form words to explain the inexplicable. There is no sugar-coating a message such as "your dad just died". We hugged, we cried, we wailed, they screamed.

My 10y/o asked, "Who is gonna look after us now Mum?". This was such a pivotal moment – I didn't know back then how important it was to all 3 of us, for me to say these words out loud: "I will. I will look after you!"

My 8y/o looked at me through his stream of tears and claimed, "I'm only 8 and I'm not gonna have a Daddy anymore!" it pierced through my heart – even now, writing this 4 years later, it still brings tears to my eyes.

Rob and I were "that couple". Still happily in Love after 12 years of marriage, 13 years together. Our Love started as a spark that kept burning brighter by each year. We already were a close-knit family. Yet this very moment pulled us closer together than ever.

The following months were a blur, my brain in *functioning mode*. The same evening, we drove to my in-laws to share the gut-wrenching news. The next day we flew to Perth to identify Rob's body. Such an important and bonding moment, the 4 of us together – I could feel Rob's presence so clearly, and it was not coming from his body – yet he was in the room with us, watching us hang over his body, hugging him. We found a little bit of closure in that moment, we needed to see him.

Rob and I were lucky enough to have had some conversations around the "what if". We had always said to each other "If something was to ever happen to me, I want you to take the boys and create the happiest life possible!".

Love is simple. Love just wants you to be happy!

We arranged the funeral, celebrated his life in style – Rob would have loved it. There was so much Love and laughter in the room, everybody had heart-warming stories to share.

The *same* week of the funeral I walked our youngest down the aisle for his First Holy Communion. The entire town knew – and it felt like their stare personified and reached down my throat to squeeze my heart so tight, I could hardly breathe. Tears were running down my face as I was giving my all to smile down at Jed, who kept checking back with me.

I was so incredibly proud of him.

A week later I had a nervous breakdown in our kitchen. A little bit of bickering between the boys over brushing their teeth escalated, until I called up to them "I just need peace and quiet!" Wow. That sentence opened a valve that I couldn't close anymore. It gave me a sense of relief that left me hanging for more… and I repeated the same sentence over and over, helplessly raising the volume each time, in my desperate need of being heard, until I screamed on top of my lungs as if my life depended on it "**I just need peace and quiet!**".

I collapsed on the kitchen floor, whacking cupboard doors in a forlorn attempt to handle the vehement force, before it could tear me apart. It ended in a primal scream, an out of body experience where I watched myself falling to pieces, worrying which one of our neighbours would call the police or ambulance – in my mind I saw myself being carried away, strapped to a bed, right into a psych ward. I believe that very vision made me snap out of it.

The silence was deafening.

"The boys!!" my brain switched back on, horrified by the thought of what damage my collapse would have done to them. I dragged my body up the stairs, finding them both in my bed. I felt I had completely failed them, only weeks after their dad's passing. I sat down and we talked. My *breakdown* was a *breaking open* – so many emotions, we shared so much – and I promised that I too would find somebody to talk to.

Emily was my saviour. A positive psychologist, an angel sent to me in human form. She held space for me while I was trying to make sense of everything that had occurred over the past weeks and months. One day I talked about how overwhelming it was, being confronted with society's expectation of how I was *supposed to* be handling my grief.

After all, I had chosen to honour our promise to each other: to create the happiest life possible for the 3 of us. Emily looked at me ever so calmly and posed the question that would change our world forever: "What does grief mean to *you* Marie?"

"*Empowerment!*" I responded, to my own surprise.

I had felt an indescribable strength since Rob had died, a guidance that left nothing to chance – as if my path just appeared in front of us at every step of our way. We were so looked after, literally.

"I think I have to write a book about it", I stated to Emily.

And so I did.

4 months after Rob had passed, I wrote my Love legacy to Rob, "Loving Life after Loss".

Within hours of publishing, it had not only become an Amazon no.1 bestseller, it also ranked in the top 100 of Australia! I stared at the screen in disbelief, my name on the same list as Michelle Obama, with her book "Becoming". (Needless to say: I read it, it's brilliant!)

A couple of weeks later we boarded a plane to the Maldives, followed by 9 days on the Canary Island "La Palma" – we had embarked on a trip around the world in 60 days. I decided to take the boys away from all the first milestones without their Dad; Christmas, New Years, both their birthdays. We spent Christmas with my Mum in Austria. And right there, in my old apartment, another idea was born.

I sat in a quiet moment, walking down memory lane – the past 6 months felt so surreal. I thought of the book and how it was so well received – and I realised, I had something the world needed: **Hope**.

The same evening, I contacted a mentor I knew of back in Sydney, told him about my story and we arranged to meet upon my return. After visiting friends and family in Austria and Germany, eating escargots in Paris, catching up with a friend from Denmark, and spending Flyn's birthday at the Universal Studios in Sentosa Island, we returned to what we were trying to determine as our new normal.

Back to school for the boys – and 2 weeks later I found myself in the first of many workshops, recording my welcome video for "Loving Life after Loss", the movement.

When I officially opened its doors on 19th March 2019, it felt like jumping off the cliff and growing my wings on the way down. I trusted my inner guidance. Little did I know what was to come – yet more importantly: I had been gifted everything I needed to support me in my new venture.

An ever-growing *upwards spiral* of grieving, processing, healing and sharing was started. Everything I worked through, I turned into yet another healing opportunity for others. I shared straight from my heart; my decisions, my emotions and what I learned from them.

Meanwhile the group has attracted thousands of people, all drawn to the idea of "Loving Life after Loss", even before knowing *how* to even attempt it. We offer healing journeys, programs, retreats and VIP Days, all designed to help you heal, help you shift your perspective and allow happiness, joy and Love back into your life.

I help people discover their *hidden gifts in adversity* and let go of their need to answer the question "why" or "why me". We peel back the layers around the stigma of grief and the world's helplessness of using labels and phrases, in an attempt to name what cannot be described in words. We walk a path together that nobody thought they had chosen.

A few months after starting our movement, Flyn carefully asked "Mum, I've got something to say, but I don't know how…". I instantly felt the importance of what was to come and encouraged him to share. My heart was wide open, when he carefully progressed to say "Our lives have sort of gotten better since Dad passed…" Now my heart dropped, and I gave it my all to not reflect that in my face. I looked at him in anticipation when he continued "…it's not *because* he died; it's because of what *you made of it!*".

A wave of Love rushed right through me. I could feel Rob's approval in every single one of Flyn's words. We hugged, and I knew we were on the right path. It was such a sacred moment – and I am grateful for Flyn's blessing to be sharing it with you.

I believe in Soul Contracts. Realising that Rob and I had chosen this path on a soul level, was not only one of my biggest gifts in adversity, it also gave me so much peace; it highlighted my purpose – but most of all, it highlighted the indescribable Love that Rob had for me – before, during and after our lifetime together.

I have no words to say how blessed I am to have experienced such Love.

BIO:

Marie Alessi is a mother to two boys, a bestselling Author, Legacy Coach & TEDx Speaker. After her husband passed from a brain aneurysm, she actively created her way back to Joy. She instinctively knew it was the only path worthy for their young boys. Rob had taught her the concept of two choices – and this one was made in his honour; to continue his legacy.

Marie has become a shining example of choosing Love over fear and sadness.

In her movement "Loving Life after Loss" Marie offers hope, healing and happiness to the world, when expected the least and needed the most.

www.MarieAlessi.com

3
FIND YOUR PATH AND LISTEN TO YOUR SOUL

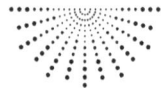

Yvette Taylor

It is 11:32am on Sunday morning, my sweaty clothes stuck to me, staring at my friends with one eye open - *'Can someone just call 'J', I need another line!'*. The room is spinning, with my mind still replaying the heavy Drum and bass set from last night over and over inside my head!

As I lay there wracked with guilt torn between feeling like a fraud and still running from the drama and trauma of my childhood and loving the little escape from reality. Yet that feeling crept in again because tomorrow I'd be back with my clients, healing their energy, advising them on supplements and helping them change their life. Once again lying to myself that I even practised what I preached!

There I was 25 years old, in a nice house, married with my own wellbeing business. I 'should' have been happy, everyone else thought my life was perfect! Yet I felt dead, dark and miserable because I knew in my heart there was more to life than what I was living!

One day it all snapped inside of me, after 8 years of lying to myself, I left my husband and business, my friends and family, packed the car and moved hundreds of miles away to restart my life. All I had was what was in the boot and a pull in my heart to take the leap. It felt as if life was controlling me to make it happen, yet I knew it was the right time to begin a new chapter.

New Beginnings

I *thought* I had dealt with my past and started to look more to my future, where I wanted to go and what I wanted to do. So I did what I always did and pushed all my energy into my career. Juggling 3 businesses, studying a full-time Acupuncture degree and working all hours to earn the money. I still believed that 'happiness' and 'success' were wrapped in the ideal lifestyle. I was driven by a need to prove to everyone from my past that I could be successful. I would have the car, the home, the holidays, the marriage and finally live the 'happy ever after'. Yet still my heart was screaming to me that this was not the way, that I was off purpose yet I didn't know what IT was and nor did I pay attention to the signs.

Somehow believing I could be the one exception, I ignored the clear signs from the universe that this was all out of flow, quieting the voices in my head with wine and chocolate and more work. I pushed and pushed, sacrificing my happiness, health and well-being along the way. It was not long before it all collapsed.

In just three weeks two businesses disappeared. Leaving me with £40k debts. With no way to pay it back. Despite everything I had been through, this felt like my rock bottom, not for me, but because I felt I had let everyone down. I felt as though I had failed and could not see a way out.

Finding Your Flow

From this place, there was no choice. I had to go back to what I knew: my energy work. Instead of focusing on building my life from the outside, again I had to go within to change how I felt. I had to find a way to release the energy of debt, small-thinking, and stop focusing on what I lost to create my future. Using energy tools I aligned my energy, thoughts, and emotions with what I wanted to do, so that everything was working WITH me.

Then I only did things which were in alignment with my vision and what I was called in my heart to do. As I started to put the beginnings of EAM (Energy Alignment Method) into practice and follow the steps to rebuild my life, I became more congruent, and my ability to attract money grew. Yet I still ignored the call in my heart to share this energy work, empower people so they can live their life purpose and ACTUALLY change the world for the better. I still felt too ashamed to come out of the spiritual closet. I would secretly work with my clients on their energy in the guise of an online marketer.

In 2014 I became happily pregnant with the little baby I was told I would never conceive. Having used the beginnings of EAM and energy healing to do so much work on myself, my hara, my health, and allowing myself to be in flow. Life just felt so exciting thinking about the amazing future that was to come. Just 6 weeks before he was born my third business failed, losing another £70k!

THIS time I paid attention to the signs from the universe! Now for many this would have been devastating yet I was thrilled. It felt like the biggest gift. Now I was free to spend time with the little one, to listen to my heart and to pursue my passion.

Whilst I sat at home with no money left and no source of income, I had no stress, no worries, no business or commitments, and no idea what to do next. I was just able to be present.

I had allowed myself to stop the 'PUSH' of life. To be honest, I had no choice but to just sit and receive.

During that time, I received download after download. I would wake in the night to scribble down notes, as pieces of the puzzle came together and EAM - The Energy Alignment Method® as we know it today was born.

As I was truly connected to this voice inside I realised I had been living my purpose and following my passion to help others change their lives all along. That is what I knew I was here for. As I stared into the eyes of my gorgeous little boy, I remember saying out loud to the universe, 'Right, if I am taking away any time from this beautiful little man it has to be the thing that I am here for. I am not f****** around anymore!'. I wanted to make a difference in the world *for him*.

Just 4 months after he was born I began sharing my passion for energy. The inner voices crept in nagging, 'Who are you to be doing this?'. 'You don't have the flashy house/ car/ lifestyle'? 'You're not 'qualified' enough' and 'What if people say that you're wrong?'. Yet the feedback from others was incredible, every day I received emails and messages from people saying how much it had transformed and changed their lives. I finally felt that I was in flow.

Letting Go with EAM

My journey to self-love, alignment and changing my life began way before EAM was born. Despite all the work I had done on myself with other methods once I began working with EAM I was able to create much bigger shifts, transform and let go of the stuckness I still felt. If ONLY I'd had this to guide me along the way sooner I know how quickly my life would have changed!

Here are the lessons I learnt along the way:

- **Pay Attention To The Universe!** - When life stops you in your tracks time and time again pay attention, you're on the wrong path. This is a course correction. It's happening FOR you never TO YOU.
- **Understand Your Life Path** - Where things repeat they are probably part of your life path to overcome these themes you need to do the energy work to change it or else it will come back again.
- **Listen To The Calling In Your Soul** - It is always there to guide you, it wants the best for you, you never have to explain yourself to anyone or question why you are doing it. Trust yourself.
- **Let Go Of People Faster** - As you go on the journey you will need help, like everything, people will come and go. Free yourself of team members who are out of alignment sooner, no need to battle with those who are misaligned with your vision!
- **You Deserve It All** - You deserve to feel and experience everything you want in life, to feel better than you do, to experience that expansion and have it be your norm, to find flow and create magical manifestations in your life.
- **Do It Anyway** - Just because there is someone doing something 'like' you, no one will do it the same AS you. No matter how big their following, their reach or who they know. YOU are here to impact the lives of those who are waiting for you, know that you have the answer to it!
- **Money Never Defines You - It Will Come & Go** - Make money doing what you love, hold high standards and be in integrity with yourself. You will never please everyone, never allow it to define you because money is transient. That said, make sure you focus on having a positive powerful relationship with

wealth because it is a wonderful energy to help you along your path, deal with your money stuff.
- **Stay True To Your Vision** - Sometimes we share our dreams with too many people too early, they lose faith or forget. Yet when you follow your heart you can trust that your big dream is there, it will come, just allow it to grow when it's ready. Keep faith in your vision, allow it to develop and follow the path to where it is meant to be.

If only I could go back to that younger me explain what these lessons from the universe meant along the way. I can see how much quicker life would have changed. Whilst it used to be my story it is no longer the basis of who I am. I no longer operate from this place; I am still on the journey to becoming. We all are and always will be.

A New Journey

I know now that I had to experience the suffering and setbacks of my childhood, it made me the woman I've become. Without that pain I would never have started on the journey of self-discovery. Without that EAM would never have been born. I know we have all been on our own journey.

Everything we have experienced is because we are strong enough to take it. There are lessons in your past who have made you who you are. In the many empowering stories in this book, you will find the gift in your journey too.

When you follow your life path, follow your heart, trust yourself and your intuition magical things can happen. Now I changed my life and thousands of others have changed theirs too with EAM and by understanding the power we hold inside.

You may have heard this all before, this time please hear it, EAM is empowering so many people just like you. Read our research studies with over 17,000+ people with amazing results. Now it's an internationally recognised complementary therapy too. If I had never followed my heart none of this would have happened. I know there is so much more to come too.

So, whatever you do, TRUST the guide inside you, tap into your inner knowing and trust that the right things will unfold for your path when you are in alignment with your truth.

BIO:

Yvette Taylor Creator of EAM - The Energy Alignment Method - a transformational self-help tool, and founder of the We Changed The World Foundation. Over the last 7 years, taken EAM globally with over 50,000+ people in 41 countries by helping them find and release limitations and reprogram their energy, thoughts, beliefs and emotions, to change their life.

She also empowers others to transform their lives so they can create business they love that changes people, communities and situations on the planet. Whatever you do, never take Yvette on in a dance competition, she will beat you every time.

www.energyalignmentmethod.com

4
LICKETY SPLIT

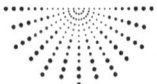

Leanne Wheeler

It all started by chance ... I found myself single in my late twenties, and ended up buying a little flat. It was modest and dated, but I loved it. The previous owner was an old lady, so it was full of things like sunflower tiles in the bathroom and lots of lavender and magnolia. I set about updating it. It was just about the time the internet was becoming mainstream (I'm so old!!) but even so, there was little information about decorating. So, I had to do my research through books and by asking tradespeople, and then by trial and error.

But I discovered that I loved it. I loved making the flat my own. I loved the creativity. And I loved the satisfaction it gave me. But because I was having to learn as I went along, it took me a looooooong time. At that point, I was in a corporate job and becoming increasingly dissatisfied with the lack of fulfilment. I was asked to relocate to London for my role, so had to rent out my flat whilst I continued to work.

This was my first experience of letting a property. I wrote the contract myself and, although I asked an agency to help find the tenants, I also managed the property myself, dealing with any issues remotely. By this point, I knew what I really loved was working on houses, but not realising it at the time, I also loved dealing with tenants. I loved helping them make somewhere their own. I talked with my father about it, and we eventually decided to buy a property together and do it up. At this point, all I wanted to do was work on refurbishing.

I searched for my perfect project. After some time, I found it – a rundown, five-bedroom house that desperately needed love! We embarked on turning it around. We completed the refurbishment and I advertised for some tenants. Again, I wrote the contract myself. It was located within a mile of the university, so it was ideal for students. Once they were confirmed, I sold the house and made £60,000, as I was able to sell it as a going concern with guaranteed rent for the year.

Once this was sold, I was able to use the money to buy more properties. I bought a smaller three-bed for me to do up and live in, and a separate larger refurb project. This was a bigger challenge. It was an old Victorian terraced house, which had been left almost untouched since the day it was built.

Two old ladies had lived in it and had done very little to it other than install a shower in a backroom and gas central heating. There was no proper bathroom – just an outside toilet inhabited by spiders, next to the old coal shed – and no proper kitchen. There was just an old scullery with a few units in, an old gas cooker and a sink. I was very lucky to get a mortgage on it! But it was the perfect next project ...or so I thought!

That was 2007, and the day the purchase completed was actually the day of the run on Northern Rock, when everyone was pulling out their money. I had bought the house with very little left to actually do the refurbishment with (novice mistake) and so had planned on borrowing the money to get the work done. However, as the market began to change, the money dried up – no one was lending, so I ended up having to fund it on my credit cards.

At the same time, I was made redundant!

Whilst for a lot of people this would have been a nightmare, in retrospect, it was the perfect outcome for me.

At least I thought so.

I had the freedom to pursue my property projects, but I didn't seem to notice at the time the lack of income. But I was able to spend my time decorating the property, and I found that I loved being on site with all the other trades. Every day was different, and I was always learning something new. I loved it!

But money was tight. All the time the property was being renovated, I was spending money either on materials or tradespeople, and nothing was coming in to replace it. I was building up more and more debt on my credit cards, to try to get the project done and the house back on the market. I had to let all the rooms in my own house.

I was living with three student nurses who all had the most palatial rooms (I made sure they were all decorated nicely so they would let easily) while I lived in the box room. It was in no means glamorous. And, whilst I was loving the fact that I was my own boss, I was seriously running out of money. Every time I paid for something – food, my decorating materials – I had a secret panic, wondering if my card would be declined. But I was in too deep now. I had to have the determination and faith to see it through.

By the time I had finished the Victorian property, the market had dried up. There was no one to sell it to. I was in a sticky situation at this point, as I'd completely run out of money. I remember collapsing in tears on my bedroom floor, wondering what the hell I was going to do. I'd put the house on the market for a big 'launch' day and there were only two viewings and definitely no offers. The market was well and truly dead. I was in despair. I remember seriously thinking I would have to declare myself bankrupt.

After a lot of tears and soul-searching, I realised I was going to have to face this somehow. I was stuck in my box room without the fun and excitement of being on site. It was a very lonely and sad place to be, having the weight of all this debt on my shoulders and an empty house, valued very highly but essentially unsaleable. I sat on my bed and listed all my debts. I started to write letters to my creditors to explain to them that I had run out of money, but that I would be able to pay them if they could give me a little time.

This took some of the pressure off, although I hadn't figured out exactly how I was going to pay them! The original plan of course was that selling the house would clear it and leave me with a chunky profit for all my hard work. But all the time the property wouldn't sell, that was no plan at all!

But then, out of the blue, I had a call from an estate agent asking if I'd consider letting the property? They said they had a family who were looking to rent in the area. They were offering rent at £1,800. My mortgage was £1,100. This was a saviour for me! Not only would they cover the mortgage, but I'd also have some profit! This way I could begin to chip away at some of the debt. The deal was done and they moved in.

Not being able to recover my money on the house by selling it, I had to go back into corporate life!

There was no choice.

I had £40,000 of credit card debt to pay off – this was money that had been used to fund the refurbishment on the house. However, by then, my mind was made up and my heart was set on working for myself. So, during this final, enforced episode of employment, I spent my evenings and weekends getting qualified as a decorator. I continued to chip away at my debts, paying them off one by one. Each time it was a step closer to living my dream life. I worked out that if I could fill the time in between refurbishing my own properties by decorating other people's houses, I could secure my own income.

10th July 2010 was a red-letter day. I left my job, packed my car in London and headed home to Hampshire. I had to live in my sister's spare room whilst I built up my business. It felt like that box room all over again, but I knew the sacrifice would one day pay off.

I took an advert out in the local paper. I volunteered to do some painting work for a local school, which was a great publicity in the parent community. Slowly, the phone began to ring. I hadn't a clue how to quote for work or how to write up specs, but I kept plugging away, just refining my processes each time. I spoke to a lot of other decorators and made a point of chatting to staff in DIY stores, to get an understanding of the business.

I lost money on some jobs in the early days, but on others I made a bit of profit, and I kept getting more customers through referrals and recommendations. Each time I had a great review or a recommendation from a customer, I'd celebrate it in some small way – either with a glass of wine or treating myself to a new bit of kit!

Over the years, as my reputation grew, I was invited to do more elaborate and different jobs. I've been able to work with some amazing interior designers, as well as some proper old school decorators, who taught me how to hang £5,000 silk panels in elaborate mansions in London! I've hand-painted beautiful kitchen cabinets right through to artistic murals and marble effects on Georgian pillars. Each time, I've approached the job with the same enthusiasm and willingness to learn.

A decade on, I cannot believe how much I've achieved. During my time decorating, I was able to go back and revisit my property journey to keep building my portfolio. I later re-mortgaged the Victorian property, which freed up enough cash to buy another house and so the portfolio has been building in the background. I now focus on letting properties to a variety of tenants and still love offering them beautiful places to stay.

The Victorian property that I mentioned, which was always bought to sell rather than to let, has actually just been sold for £800,000, which makes the box room experience definitely worth it!

It's strange that at times life can seem so bleak and hopeless, but it turns out that, just by hanging on in there with a bit of determination, things can very much turn a corner and come good. More so than you can ever have expected.

If you have a passion for something – as I discovered that I had for decorating and property – don't be afraid to turn it into a business. There will be distractions – there may even be disasters – but there will definitely be a way through – a way to turn that passion into a profession.

BIO:

Leanne Wheeler is a painter and decorator working in Winchester under the name Leanne's Lick of Paint. She is trained professionally and has worked on a variety of projects from heritage buildings and full-scale renovations to upcycling and transforming pieces of furniture. This has involved everything from exterior and interior painting, using a variety of finishes, wallpaper hanging, wood staining, varnishing and upcycling techniques such as decoupage. Leanne has just launched her Masterclass which teaches you the basics on how to transform any room in your house (available on her website).

In her spare time (when not trying to decorate her own home!) Leanne loves to spend time with her two children, running and enjoying the odd glass of red wine in the garden.

www.leanneslickofpaint.co.uk

5
AFTER IT FALLS APART

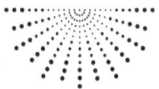

Kirsty Carden

It was Sunday the 23rd November 2014, the day after my 30th birthday celebration. I was in the dining room of our new Edwardian home. It needed a full renovation, but I loved it. There she was by the brick chimney fireplace, looking so happy, ironing and speaking about how proud she was of her sons. Her son was my husband and she was my mother-in-law, Sue.

I really hit gold when it came to mother-in-laws. Have you ever met someone who is so positive, joyful and has an energy you just love to be around? That was Sue.

Sue loved kids and was an amazing mother and grandmother. She left us later that day to see her new grandchild who had just been born.

A couple of weeks later, I called her up and to my surprise, she wasn't communicating properly. She couldn't talk or think in the same way and passed the phone to my father-in-law, who was worried about her. What I haven't yet mentioned was that

Sue had terminal cancer. She had suffered with it for 5 years, yet always continued on. We had done so much over those years from holidays, to both her sons getting married, her meeting her first grandchildren etc. Yet all of a sudden, things were different. I told my husband that he needed to contact his mum and that she didn't sound right. We were later told things had suddenly deteriorated and the cancer had spread. It was cutting off oxygen to her brain. She didn't have much time left. As soon as we were told we decided that we would leave early the next morning to be with her. At 6:15am that same morning we got a call, Sue had passed.

This was the moment that everything started to change.

Over the coming months, we mourned Sue. My husband was diagnosed with reactive depression. At work I was taken away from the people and office I knew and put into another, where my role started to change. My ability to work from home was also taken away and I had never felt so alone.

Losing my mother-in-law made me realise how short life is and how I needed to change things I'm not happy about right now. It made me also see that through hard times, you can remain positive and you can live a good life (something I had never seen demonstrated till that point). So, I began my search for my own purpose.

Yet, at the same time, it created problems in my own marriage with my husband and myself both mourning Sue and feeling very different about life.

Then, on the 16th September, everything came to a massive halt. This was the day that I decided I was not going back to work, back to the same life, I decided to fully commit to making myself, my relationship with my husband and my own purpose and career, everything it should be!

I had been contemplating what it was I really wanted to do for a while. I had worked in the media industry for many years, but I felt that it wasn't what I was ultimately meant to do. I came from a background I was very different from, both mentally and physically and I had 'thought' my way out of it, getting into environments that would help transform me. At 16 I went to a college where there were halls so I could stay and study, and this was the start of great things. Where I went on to get A Grade A-Levels in Sociology, Communication Studies and Media.

I then went on to University to continue my journey. I was determined to be a success and to make something of myself to then carry that through to the next generation.

So when I discovered I was pregnant in my second year of University, it was a massive shock. Everyone thought I would need to quit university and that my dreams were over, but I refused to believe that.

I could do both, I could complete my degree and have a baby and guess what, I did!

Years later, I became a single mum (by choice) while building my career in Media and then met the man of my dreams! My now husband and partner of 13+ years (side note: I knew I was going to marry him from the first week, so that stuff they say about knowing you met the one is true!).

And the thing I was always fascinated with, read, studied, watched, was human behaviour. I had always wondered how is it you can grow up in an environment where everyone is one way and thinks the same, yet you can be so totally different?

How can some people be so positive even when they have the worst news, like my mother-in-law, yet others be so negative?

I would naturally get the best out of people and they would open up to me, I loved talking and being there for others and loved motivating and challenging people for their benefit.

So I was exploring different careers, should I be a psychologist? A politician? A life coach...?

And just like that a friend's girlfriend became a life coach, so

I really got to learn about it and for once everything clicked. This is exactly what I want to do. It related to everything I had ever done with my own life and others, my interests, my studies. It was flexible, I could work from anywhere and I could really help people and make a difference!

I knew this was what I wanted to do - I felt it!

There is a saying that goes 'When the pupil is ready the teacher will appear' and they did!

I found a programme to join to become a certified coach and learn all there is about online business. However it was $14,500!!

I was quitting my job, we had just bought a house that needed a full renovation, I had a young son, a mortgage and had just gone through hell the last year emotionally.

For many people these would be reasons NOT to do it, for me these were reasons TO do it!

However, where was I going to get that money from?

To find it, I completely shifted my perspective on how I would achieve my goals and did something that would change my life forever.

Instead of saying 'I can't afford it/do it' I said 'How can I afford it/do it'?

And just like that the ideas came...

I used some of my savings, I cashed in some shares, yet there was still a chunk left, £8,400 to be precise. So I applied for an interest free credit card. And guess what the exact amount was on there? £8,400. If I needed a sign, that was it!

I was in! I told my husband (I was so nervous) but he supported and trusted me, so we came up with a plan. He agreed that whilst I was starting out, he would pay the bills and I would pay my half of the mortgage. But with no income yet, I had to get resourceful. So, I rented out the spare room, which covered my half while I was building the business and worked out exactly how long I would have till I needed to make money, which was June that year.

And guess what happened? The programme started late January and by June I was ready to bring in the clients and they came in!

I knew in order for me to step into my next level I needed the container to do this. How would I know how to sell online or find clients when I had never done that before? How else would I become a coach without doing the qualification and 100 hours to make it happen?

I created what I now call a 'Success Container'. It's the thing that stretches you, it's something you commit time, energy and investment in, so that it happens!

We often don't take action unless we have to, which is why I am such a huge fan of coaching, mentorship and training, because when we invest, we are invested.

So where are things now?

My first year in business I got fully booked with clients, I created a digital product and at the end of that year I created my first small mastermind event (I've run these ever since).

My confidence grew massively and things I was terrified of, like public speaking, I faced and became confident in, I grew a community of women and started to feel whole. I was living my purpose! I was travelling every 3 months for work to the most amazing locations (Miami, LA, Florence, Paris..).

I started more as a general life and purpose coach, but as my business grew in success and I enjoyed business so much I niched down to supporting women in business grow online, building their confidence, creating their amazing communities and helping them become part of one!

I then went on to create a mastermind of my own after the first year, which I still run to today (it's evolved since).I started an Online business training Academy for women a year after that, which is now CPD Accredited.. I have multiple digital products like my content creation system. I run events and speak. My podcast TRANSFORM with Kirsty Carden topped the self help charts on its release (even ahead of Tony Robbins) and my audience has grown to over 50,000.

My business has hit more than a million in revenue with great profits, as it's mostly grown organically.

However it has not all been easy! I have had bad experiences with mentors and team members saying they do one thing, but doing something else. A huge lack in ethics and integrity. All of this has simply motivated me to create something better!

I have had a couple of challenging clients that have triggered me and hurt me, yet all of this helps you learn where you need to grow and heal.

From every bad experience I have learnt something and I continue to do so.

I am now upgrading both my Mastermind and my Academy so that they are more holistic, incorporate more alignment, thereby helping women to do business THEIR way. I'm bringing in better certifications for coaching and business.

My biggest piece of advice for someone starting out is this: If you know you want to do it, then you need to start asking yourself 'How?' As soon as you ask that question a part of your brain will find the answers for you! As soon as you think you can't, you shut this down!

And the next piece of advice is: invest in a 'Success Container' to support you.

Think of it like this; If a goldfish is put in a small bowl it will only grow to the size of that bowl. If you put the same goldfish into a larger pond, it will grow much much larger, to fit that container. It's the same for you!

What larger container can you get into to support your growth? Who or what can support you? Think of training programmes, people, mentors and environments. At the end of the day, we are all products of the environment we are in because:

"When a flower doesn't bloom you don't change the flower, but the environment of which it is in"

Remember you are the flower (even if you're covered in soil) so go get in the right environment NOW, so you can fully bloom to your greatest potential!

BIO:

Kirsty Carden is a Business Coach, Certified NLP Master & Mindset Coach & Speaker. She is the host of the chart topping Self Help Podcast TRANSFORM with Kirsty Carden. For over 6 years Kirsty has worked with 100s of aspiring and current female entrepreneurs, putting them in the environment for success and confidently growing profitable aligned businesses online. As well as being a CPD registered training company offering online business certifications.

www.kirstycarden.com

6
BEHIND THE MASK

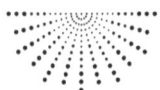

Rebecca Hallam

When I was first asked to write a chapter for this book, I didn't think I had much to say. Of course, there is a story behind my business and me as a person. But I wasn't really sure if anyone would really care. It's not really your typical entrepreneur journey, it gets a bit dark and a bit gritty, and I know that can be too much for some people to handle. But I talked to a few people and I realised it's an important story to tell. Because not all businesses are born from good places. Some are born from the pits of despair and take work to climb out of before they can blossom into something beautiful.

That's what I learned in my journey and what I want to share with you. So be warned, I don't sugar-coat. I'll always be honest about my struggles in life, and about how it got me to where I am now.

Where It All Began

If you don't mind, I'm going to skip over the formative years of my life. Let's just say my childhood was traumatic and it set me down a bad path for the next 20 years or so.

I've always struggled with my mental health. I was diagnosed as bipolar at 15, which presented a lot of challenges in my young life and still does now. The combination of mental illness and childhood trauma meant that I looked for a way to cope, and I was drawn to drugs. It was an incredibly dark time for me, and something that I struggled with for many years. Addiction is a strange thing – it strips you of your passions and consumes your life. For example, I've always loved horses, and as a young girl I was riding for the under 16s Olympic Dressage team. But when I started using and selling drugs my chance slipped away, and eventually, I ended up working in my dad's garage selling cars instead. It was a stable job that I was good at, but I still felt very lost. When my relationship failed, I found myself sitting on the floor asking myself "what the hell am I going to do with my life?".

Recovery And Makeup

My childhood wasn't exactly pretty or pleasant, but it did give me one thing. It sparked my love for special effects makeup. I started experimenting with it when I was young, and special effects makeup really called to me. I loved the fact that in just 30 minutes or so I could change who I was in the mirror, and I could be someone else for a little while; someone I wasn't. That stuck with me, and it's something I'm very passionate about to this day.

When I got to that very low point, I decided I needed to get clean. I went to a rehab facility in Argentina where you work on a ranch as part of your recovery. This was really therapeutic for me, being around something I loved and grounding me in the real world. While I was there, I had a lot of time to think, and that question kept bouncing around my head. What am I going to do with my life? What do I love? Then one day it hit me – I've got to start up my own business, and it's got to be a makeup business.

The Birth Of Peekaboo

One thing you might not know about people with bipolar is that we're very impulsive. One day after I arrived home, I was walking through our town centre, and I saw a vacant shop with a sign advertising for tenants. I knew I had to take it then and there. No planning or anything like that, I just called the agent and signed the papers.

My friends and family were incredibly supportive, even though I'm pretty sure they thought I was nuts at the time. One of my closest friends even helped me name it – Peekaboo. I've always been called Becky Boo (personalised license plate and everything), so Peekaboo seemed like a good fit, even if it did sound a bit like a sex shop! I launched Peekaboo Hair and Makeup studio, doing professional makeup, SFX and selling makeup.

Rock Bottom

You might think that everything went swimmingly from there. I'd been to rehab, I had a business, and I had customers. But behind the scenes was a different story. Addiction is like a monster that always has its claws in you, trying to pull you back down into the dark depths at a moment's notice. It was a constant struggle, and the business wasn't going well. But I was still showing up every day, fighting the addiction, and I saw that as a positive.

Then my world was torn apart. About a year after I opened

the shop, my partner Joe died from a drug overdose. This was without a doubt one of the hardest things I've ever been through, and there's no nice way to say this, but I went absolutely off the rails. My life as I knew it felt pointless and dark. I stopped going to work, the shop was shut all the time and I didn't know if I could afford to pay rent from one month to the next. I stopped talking to people, and I just didn't care about anything. During this time I also had something called an ischemic stroke and my nose collapsed. It felt as though this was the end of the road for me.

But I felt guilty for thinking that. I knew that, if someone were to look at my life from the outside, it seemed like I had everything. I had horses, I owned my own house, and I had a business with a lot of potential. But my bipolar was the worst it had ever been and I was struggling with it daily. I was grieving for my lost partner, and I just couldn't see a purpose in my life anymore.

My best friend and her husband, who have been there for me since day one, sat me down one day and had a stern talk. I couldn't be like this anymore. I was killing myself in front of them, and it was a waste. That struck a bit of a chord for me, and I had something like an epiphany.

Despite all of the trauma and struggles, I had always been a determined and driven person. I was successful in everything I'd done, even in the grip of addiction, and I realised I had to succeed at this too. I got myself out of the hole I was in, I had to make the studio work, or I was going to be dead.

Now, I haven't touched drugs or alcohol in 5 years. I made a commitment to myself that I would never do it again, for Joe, and for me. To symbolise that, I had my nose reconstructed, and that started me on a new journey, and towards a new face for Peekaboo.

New Beginnings

From that point on, I wanted to do just one thing; create a safe space for everyone who walked through my doors. No fears of being judged, or not belonging or of inadequacy. I wanted Peekaboo to be a place for anyone who might be struggling with these things, or anything really, to come and feel welcome, supported and special.

I started training, practising, and taking the business seriously. I stopped selling makeup and turned the shop into an actual beauty studio, somewhere people can come and feel amazing. I poured everything I had into the business – I even joke that my new drug is business! With the support and love of my friends and the community, the studio grew, and I did too.

Now I've won dozens of awards for my work (including Entrepreneur of the Year), I've done makeup and special effects in Hollywood films (you might have seen my work in 'The Witches' or 'Mama Mia'), and I've levelled up into a better version of myself.

But along with the makeup, there was another area I wanted to grow into. I have a very addictive personality, and after Joe died, I turned to food. I put on a lot of weight, and I became really unhappy with myself as a result. During lockdown, I decided enough was enough. I lost seven stone during the pandemic by kickboxing, riding and using Saxenda. In January 2022, I treated myself to full body liposuction, a boob job and a fair amount of facial work. It cemented all of my hard work and made me feel like myself again – only healthier.

That's what inspired me to start training as a nurse practitioner - to be able to offer aesthetic services to my clients. To give people control over their lives and help them bring their inner beauty to the surface. Aesthetics gives me a way to make a real, positive difference to people's lives, and that's incredibly important to me.

During the pandemic, I also launched two new businesses.

The first was a new product called a Boo Box – a subscription box of false eyelash products that could be shipped directly to your door. This took off in ways I just hadn't expected, with 2000 lashes sold in the first hour! Influencers like Jeffree Star have used them, and they inspired the 'House of Boo' product brand. The second was a wine bar, called 10 Station Road, which (once the pandemic restrictions started to ease) became an incredible success, and is now a thriving local hot spot.

Final Thoughts

I've had people tell me I carry my past trauma and addiction around with me like a suitcase. And yes, in some ways I do, but I feel like it's really important to be honest about what goes on behind the scenes. Because when you see people on Instagram looking like they live perfect lives and run amazing businesses, it can be discouraging. But life isn't really like that. There's dirt and trauma, and you never know what someone has gone, or is going through.

What all of that showed me, and I hope it can show you too, is that it doesn't matter what background you're from or what you've gone through. If you have a passion, you can start a business and make it a success – and you should! You only get one life, and you should spend it doing something you love. Success isn't something you're born with, or something only the privileged can achieve. It's out there for everyone if you're willing to put in the work.

So no, I'm not your typical business success story. Yes, my business is successful, but I've clawed with bleeding nails to get where I am today. I could just as easily not be here at all. I'm incredibly grateful for the second chance I've had in life, and I plan to do everything I can with it. That includes a lot of work with local charities, raising thousands of pounds for causes I care about and giving all I can back to the community that has given me so much.

No matter where you are in life you can always turn things around, become something new and achieve anything you put your mind to. After all, I'm living proof. Don't ever feel confined to the way things are, because that's what society wants or what social media says you should be. Don't let yourself be put in a box because it makes them more comfortable. Follow your passions, give it your all and put your unique stamp on the world.

Why fit in when you were born to stand out?

BIO:

Becky is the owner and driving force behind Peekaboo Studio. Based in Petersfield, Peekaboo has been running for 6 years, making the transition from owner-operated beauty business, to a flourishing, multi-award-winning aesthetics clinic and beauty studio.

But the studio isn't the only thing that's transformed. As well as opening 2 more businesses (House of Boo and Station 10), owner and founder Becky has also gone through some big changes in her journey as a business owner and has trodden quite an inspirational path along the way. This chapter proves that you can succeed at absolutely anything - as long as you have passion.

www.houseofboo.net

7
THE WEIRDO IN THE ROOM

Kate Clarke

Family was the real instigator of my freelance journey. After having my twins, I knew it wouldn't be sustainable to live and work in a city. So, I began to plan what life would look like when they were at school and with my husband working away a lot. I knew freelance was the best option.

But my dream of owning my own business started way before that.

"I am not confident enough to start my own business."

I used to tell myself this story all the time, and yet in my early 20s this was all I would think about daily.

I would sit at my desk in my office job and think about what kind of business I could start. The problem was I was thinking too big. In my mind I thought I had to create some brand-new thing that no one had ever seen before. I thought starting a business was about borrowing a load of money from a bank and trying to create the next big thing.

Finding my place

As a kid I was super shy. I struggled to express myself, to make friends, to speak up, to be seen and heard, and just generally to cope in most social situations. I still have social anxiety now; I dread most social experiences.

I've always felt like the weirdo in the room, never quite fitting in anywhere.

I still don't fit in, but nowadays I don't care as much because I've found the people in my life who love me and get me.

I grew up in a small town made of lots of decent hardworking folk where I went to the local mixed comprehensive. I loved learning so I really didn't mind school at all.

I was top set for everything at school, yet I felt like a total dunce. I struggled in every class except art. This is where I shone. I loved that class. I would look forward to it all week wishing I could do art every day of the week.

I left school with a bunch of B grades and an A* in Art & Design at GCSE and A Levels in Art, IT and Design Tech.

Choosing which subject to study at university was one of the hardest decisions I've ever made. I should have done an art degree right? You would think so, wouldn't you? But no, I decided I needed to learn something that would get me a job at the end of it, and so went for Industrial Design.

Halfway through the second year I was struggling big time with the engineering knowledge needed. All I wanted to do was make things look pretty, but form over function apparently doesn't make you a great product designer. So, with no confidence in the subject when I graduated, I felt pretty lost about the future.

I had always loved fashion and thought I'd try to get into buying, only to be laughed at by a recruitment agent who quickly ushered me into an interview with a call centre.

I lasted two weeks.

After that I managed to fall into a job as a marketing

assistant in a law firm and this was the beginning of my marketing career.

I happily worked my way up for a few years while studying for my Chartered Institute of Marketing certificate and post grad diploma. Life was dreamy. I also met my future husband, moved to Manchester, and bought my first house during this time.

Then things started to change the higher up the ladder I got.

The career path I was on, was leading me to head of marketing or marketing director in a B2B company. And the thought of it made my blood run cold. I knew it wasn't what I wanted to do. Managing a team didn't excite me. But I didn't know any other way; I didn't believe I was brave enough to change direction.

And so, from that moment everything started to fall apart. I was getting complaints from colleagues that my attitude was poor. I had no energy for the job anymore. Outside of work I was having fertility problems and my marriage was falling apart. This was my rock bottom.

The stress was making the fertility worse and the lack of a baby in my life was making the rest unbearable. It was during this time I became obsessed with health, nutrition, and wellbeing.

After three years of trying for a baby, I got the go ahead for IVF and had my twins. I went back to the same company after having my babies, but I was sidestepped into a different role, with no responsibility and pretty much zero contact with any stakeholders. This suited me fine. I loved it; I was getting paid the same money to do an easier job without having to deal with any of the senior management staff. Which gave me the space to start planning the next step.

Creating the dream

So, I went back to the dream of owning my own business.

By this time, I had done some self-discovery, and with the help of a friend and pen and paper, I figured out how I could use the skills I already had. I refined what I was doing to focus on the part of the job I loved, and not do the stuff that didn't make me feel good.

I knew from my experiences that working with business owners in the wellbeing industry was where I needed to be.

There's a misconception that what happens when people decide to run their own business is that they decide to do it, then they just do it. What happens is a much longer process than that. So, if you're in this boat and you have the dream, start with the end goal in mind and know that it's going to be a bit of a journey to get there, but the universe has its way.

For me, I knew my kids would be starting school in 2020 and possibly pre-school in 2019. So that was my goal to be up and running with paying clients by September 2019. With the idea that I would replace my salary by the following year. Well, I had to have a dream!

I set out to upskill in Digital Marketing, because I knew if I was to go freelance, I'd need to have what the market wanted. I settled on a Digital Mums course in Social Media Management. The thing that swayed me to this course rather than an overarching Digital Marketing course was that at the end of the course there was a whole module on giving you the confidence and skills to become a freelancer.

It'll be easy I thought. Once I have the skills in this, I'll be ready to give up my job and throw myself in. Wrong again.

Once I graduated, I felt more lost than ever. There was still so much to learn.

I also didn't feel ready to leave the warm comfort of my salary.

So, while I was still in employment, I took a few baby steps.

Decided on a business name. Kate Clarke Marketing. Creative right!? Created a logo, set up a basic website using Wix (another mistake – Squarespace and WordPress seem to be the better options for what I needed, but little did I know). I decided on a few services to get started in social media but no real strategy for packages and pricing.

I started posting on social media randomly – again no real strategy despite the fact I'd just graduated in how to do this for clients.

The clients did not start rolling in, let me tell you. But I did start working with my best mate and absolute hero Caroline D'Arcy. She had also started her own business, in a much more trailblazing way than me, and she needed some help managing the back end of her business. Right, client one was in the bag; now to get a few more. The next few clients again came from friends and friends of friends, until I was slowly starting to build a portfolio that would help me sell myself.

I was still nowhere near ready to quit my job though!

In the end, after joining a different company which didn't work out, I was kind of forced into my freelance life. Which I guess was the only way I was going to get there. So, everything happens for a reason.

Learning from the journey

I read so many books in the lead up to taking the plunge and also soon after. My sources of inspiration came from Mel Robbins, Danielle La Porte, Eckhart Tolle, and Gay Hendricks.

It has been a journey and a half. I expected a straight linear path to get from starting out to earning decent money. The reality is it's a squiggly line that goes in different directions. You make good decisions, and you make bad ones. I realise now the aim is to make as many bad ones as you can so you can learn faster and create the success you want.

Right now, three years into the journey, I am still learning. I am not earning what I thought I would be by now, but I have had to let go of the 'should be's' and the comparisons to other business owners.

I do however have the time to do the school run every morning and be there at pick up every day if I want to be. My kids eat freshly cooked food most days and we spend time together before they go to bed every night. They are healthy and happy. This is my success right now.

My journey is far from over and I'm refining and tweaking the ideal client, package and pricing all the time and learning how to be an accountant, lawyer, and salesperson at the same time. Some days it can feel overwhelming, and some days I think it would just be easier to go get a job. But the truth is, I've put so much into this, and I couldn't let go of the freedom and autonomy I have over my life now.

The important thing I'm reminding myself of, is that it's ok to change direction, and I did just that during 2021. I stopped working with my freelance clients to help Hannah Cox launch the Better Business Network membership. I truly believed at the time this was where my future was and threw everything at it. Turns out it takes a lot longer to build a viable membership than I thought, and I went back to my business needing to build up my client base once again.

For me success is feeling like I'm making progress no matter how small. I'm learning about myself, my profession and refining my skills. I am working with my absolute dream clients who pay on time and are happy with the work I do. The best part is that I get a sense of purpose and creative output every day!

BIO:

After years of corporate stress and infertility Kate became obsessed with health and wellbeing. Now, using her experience in content marketing, Kate helps health coaches and nutritionists to have a consistent well planned out content marketing so that they can generate consistent enquiries and grow their business. Her mission is to simplify content creation and amplify the important messages of her clients.

Kate has over 15 years of marketing experience and has been self-employed since 2019, when she started Kate Clarke Marketing. She is CIM and Digital Mums qualified.

www.kateclarkemarketing.com

8
IT'S TIME TO PLAY

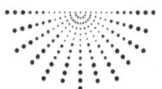

Katie Betteridge

Why work with kids? Easy – they're amazingly funny, clever, strong willed, honest, inquisitive, and stroppy! I've always loved kids, especially the younger ones. Watching their little brains ticking over when they're trying to work something out or watching other children playing. My infant school headmistress said I was going to be a teacher when I grew up; I didn't disagree with her, but even then I remember thinking, "well obviously I would be the head teacher!". Now I'm not a teacher, but I do get to play with kids every day. To give them an environment where they can learn, express themselves, use their wonderful imagination and yes have a good old strop if they want to! But also a place for parents to meet, relax, and chat with other parents knowing that their child is learning just by playing.

Looking for independence

I think I've always known that I wanted my own business, to be independent, control my own destiny. One element of my Uni course was to produce a business plan and present it to a real bank manager! I based mine on my part-time job in a fruit and veg shop. The owner, Ted, took me to the veg market at 3am to show me the ropes. In hindsight this would never have been the job for me – 3am? I'm not a morning person! I was extremely nervous meeting the bank manager and still remember the bank, the winding staircase up to the bank manager's office, talking through my plan, with my course lecturer sat behind me grading me. The bank manager told me a similar business plan had been presented to him the week before (no pressure then !!). At the end, he told me to come back when I finished Uni and he would give me the money. Wow! What a boost to my confidence. Yep ok then, you're on. I found a building in a nearby village that would work. But then things got real and self-doubt set in and I didn't set up my own veg shop. Instead, I worked not one, but 5 part-time jobs while I looked for my first "proper job". I sent over 150 letters to companies, trying to get an interview (as there was no internet/email in those days!), with no replies. When I finally got the job, it wasn't because of any of my qualifications, but because I was working 5 part time jobs and they knew I wouldn't be lazy. So that started my 25-year career in shipping!

As my husband tells me quite often, I have been very lucky to have had a job (and now two!) that I love. A job that I want to get out of bed for. That I enjoy going to. Where I like the work AND the people. But that's what I had. I worked hard. It wasn't an important job in the grand scheme of things, not like brain surgery, but sometimes it felt like it. It was an extremely busy environment with lots of technical and legal parts to it. It was 24/7. As I was a grafter, I was given more work and projects. After all, if you want something done, ask a busy person! I wasn't upset about this. I loved the work, loved knowing how everything fitted together, loved projects where you would get a say on the outcome. I've always wanted to be "needed", to be organising things, to know the answer.

Proving myself

My first chance of management came after a couple of years. At the time, the Commercial management team in our company was all male and all a generation older than me. I was very excited and nervous, but I remember a member of the team, Jeremy, telling me that I shouldn't have got the job, Scott should have – he had been there longer and was the Managing Director's son. I tried not to take offence, but it hurt. It made me harder on myself; I needed to prove that a woman could do this job. It didn't help that I'm also a natural blonde. People didn't dye their hair so much 25 years ago, so a blonde was actually a blonde. You know all the blonde jokes. Though they're jokes, I felt people did/do think there's an element of truth in the dumbness (it's why I never took typing at school!). There I was, young, female, and blonde, proving that I was damn good at my job.

Some months later Jeremy did actually apologise to me. He'd got it wrong. I was the right person for the job after all. I was lucky to have a job that took me to both sides of the world. Because I had knowledge of quite a few different elements of our business, I was ideally placed to get involved in projects. I loved visiting colleagues in different countries. Working together to find logical, workable solutions to problems. When in Japan I was called up by my daughter to ask where her school skirt was – the group I was working with thought it was great that I could just switch back to mum mode, and even though I was on the other side of the world, I still had the solution to her problem!

Finding family-work balance

My kids mean the world to me. I've always wanted a family the size of the Waltons (if you're young, Google them!), living on Walton's Mountain. I had a good career and wanted kids. Can't I have both? Does society say I can't have both? Does it make me a bad and selfish mother to want to keep my career but still have children? Kids grow up so fast and before I know it they won't need me; then what will I be left with? Shouldn't my girls see that if you work hard you can achieve. During maternity leave with my second daughter I got involved with the PTA. I was desperate to use my brain! Being a mother was a busy job, but it wasn't the type of work I was used to – I needed to be stretched. Despite that, social pressure and how I viewed myself got the better of me, and I went part time after our second daughter. It meant I had to give up my manager role, company car and a chunk of my salary. But I did it. On my days off, I got stuck into my PTA role which meant working closely with the school and of course the amazing children. It was lovely and I really enjoyed it.

So, spring forward a few years and I was back into "Head of department" mode and in a job that I never thought I'd leave unless it was in a wooden box! But you never know what life is going to throw at you do you?

Finding independence

"Your department is moving to our head office in Sweden". What? How did that happen? We had just spent two years moving all the European work to us. Why did they want to move it now? We were finally getting there after all the blood, sweat, and tears (yep all three from me!). So the big question was: do I stay, or do I go? It was one of the hardest decisions I have ever made. As I grappled with it, I realised my dream of running my own business could be possible. I would have a chunk of money to help start it up. I wanted to do something with children obviously, soft play or even role play maybe? Working hard for myself rather than for someone else. Making decisions that I don't have to check with x number of people. But the responsibility. What if I failed? What if no one wanted to come to my new business? We could lose our house. If I stay, I know the job, I get paid regularly, and I love the people I work with. It was a tough decision. It made me quite ill – pains in my chest, mammograms – which seems crazy as I was used to a lot of pressure. The emotional turmoil of not knowing what to do – should I? Shouldn't I? I just had to have faith in myself. My husband was (and still is) amazing and he had enough faith in me for the both of us! So I put a business plan together and worked out what this might cost. I could do this! I actually could be my own boss. I just needed to grow a pair. I'm a hard worker, I can do this. I eventually found a building. The potential landlord (a large supermarket) wanted to meet me, to check I was "capable" since I hadn't run a business before. I didn't take offence. I knew I was new to this, but I also knew my business plan was good and thorough. Luckily, they agreed. So that's when my switch from employee to employer began. I believe if you have the right ethos you can do it. Do I know what I am doing? Absolutely not. Am I willing to learn and try? Absolutely yes. I've taken my experience from my shipping career and transferred it to my role play village. Different businesses but there are a lot of transferable skills that I use now. Maybe you have skills you don't realise you have that were developed when you were an employee.

What I've learnt

That was just over two years ago, a few weeks before the first Covid lockdown. As we've been closed for over a year, does that still make us a new business? We may not have actually been going long, but I've learnt a lot. I'm not Superwoman: I can't do everything on my own. In business, it's important to have support around you. Doing this pretty much on my own, I needed a sounding board. People to bat ideas off of. You need to be open to other people's opinions. Yes, you'll make mistakes; it's trial and error, but that's all part of the learning. You may even feel that you're just blagging your way through. I'm surprised how much I worry about money. Hopefully it's just because we had a rocky start, with Covid and now with the cost of living crisis and rising energy bills. But I need to find some of the courage that I had when starting this business. It's a good business. It can succeed. It will succeed. Last night I was at a small local concert. I turned around to see two ladies behind me – one said to the other, "oh look it's the role play lady. We love role play! You are more famous than Jo O'Meara (S-Club 7 lady on stage!)". It made me quite emotional. This is what success feels like, and it feels bloody good.

BIO:

Katie Betteridge is the owner of I Wanna Be...Role Play Village in Romsey near Southampton. Nominated for the HWBG "Best Bricks and Mortar" award and Little Ankle Biters "Best New Business" and "Best Party Venue", and winner of the SME "Most Innovative Play Venue – Hampshire". She is married and a mother to two teenage daughters. She has run a women's netball team for the last 10+ years and would love to get back into ballroom dancing when she has more time!

www.iwannabe.co.uk

9
CAN YOU CHANGE THE WORLD

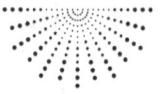

Peace Mitchell

It was like a slap across the face.
"You can't change the world you know, Peace," she said in a sarcastic huff.

Stopping me in my tracks. Quick, hot, unexpected. From out of nowhere.

Time seemed to slow down. I stared at her in disbelief as she stood there with her smug smirk, looking down at me with her arms crossed. She'd been the prettiest girl in high school at a time when I'd felt awkward and ugly. We'd never spoken to each other in those days, but now we were adults I thought we were friends. I thought we understood each other and shared the same values. Nothing made sense.

Then I remembered we weren't alone, and the rest of the women were staring at us, watching the drama unfold, waiting to see who would make the next move. It was a group project after all and they were as much invested in having their say as we were. But in that moment, it was just her and me.

I can't change the world. Really?

This was one of my deepest core beliefs. If you can do something good for someone else, you should. You always should.

Since I was a little girl, I've wanted to change the world. No, not just wanted to, I somehow believed it was what I was born to do.

That one sentence was the beginning of everything. I realised at that moment I believed I could change the world, and she was wrong. It was a shock to know not everyone thought the same way, and that we weren't all on the same page with wanting to.

It would take me another few months to know what to do with this realisation and when I look back, I remember that time so clearly.

We knew it was coming. I regretted not leaving almost immediately. We knew it was headed straight for us, we knew it was going to be big, but honestly we didn't believe it. After all, cyclones hover around off the coast and then head out to sea all the time. None of the big ones had crossed here for twenty years.

The blue skies, brilliant sunshine, community festival and celebrations of the day before had lulled us into a false sense of security. 'Everything's fine,' the sky seemed to say. 'There's no storms here, the weathermen got it wrong, there's nothing to worry about.'

But they didn't have it wrong. Not this time. We were wrong. It was our family and our community who would now pay for not heeding the warnings we were given.

The ordeal continued through the night, screaming, howling, and tearing the world apart. The unearthly roar punctuated by dramatic bursts of thunder and lightning.

Of course, I couldn't sleep. My husband called me over to

the window where he was watching the destruction unfold. Trees and branches were hurled around as if they were nothing, every leaf shredded from every tree. I was shaking but believed we were safe in the solid concrete room we had chosen to ride out the storm.

The explosion of glass was sudden and unexpected. My husband's reflexes kicked in first and he threw me to the ground before I knew what was happening. It was pitch black.

My first thought was, 'Am I covered in glass?' And then the sickening thought: 'What about the kids?'.

They were okay. Miraculously, the air pressure difference has caused the window to explode outwards and none of the shards of glass were inside. However, now the air pressure in the room intensified as the window was gone.

If I hadn't regretted staying before, I did now, why had I risked our lives? I vowed never to do this again, but it wasn't over. Not by a long way. We knew there would be hours more of this relentless destruction. In disbelief, I woke the boys and told them to hide under the bed, safely away from what was left of the window. I sang songs over and over to distract them as we waited it out in the cramped and uncomfortable space under the bed.

When it was finally over, we trudged down the road to our house, intact but with significant water damage throughout. Driving into town electrical wires were tangled, roofs had been torn from houses, farms had been flattened, and everything was broken. Our town was unrecognisable.

The shock hit us hardest. How do you come back from this scale of destruction? The structural clean up happened first. Men came out with chainsaws, tarps and tools. The army came too, along with builders from out of town, clearing roads, restoring power, and rebuilding homes. But it was the emotional damage that was harder to repair.

Thankfully, no one was killed but the grief and loss was

visible everywhere as tarps inadequately covered roofs and flapped in the depressing drizzling rain that went on for another six months. Mass scale trauma wasn't something we were used to in our idyllic tropical paradise.

We were invited to host a community morning tea for the Governor of Queensland, her Excellency Quentin Bryce. I don't know how we did it. We had no power or running water, but we made it happen. When I asked her how we could help our community to recover, she replied, 'When women are happy, well, and fulfilled, they are better able to look after everyone else.' It was such a simple statement but one that has stayed with me.

Not many people remember the day they found their calling, but I do, that one conversation was the lightbulb moment where I recognised just how important women were in holding the world together.

In the aftermath of the Cyclone, it was the mothers who were the glue holding the community together: supporting their husbands emotionally, caring for the children, checking in on elderly neighbours, helping each other to keep the wheels turning and so my sister and I and two friends focused our attention, energy and efforts on to ensuring we were finding ways to support the women of our community. We formed a non-profit organisation and held local events, fundraisers and even worked with the council and local businesses to build spaces for women to gather, care for children and connect with each other.

From a time when our whole community was lost and broken, when it seemed like the end and there was devastation all around us, we discovered the hope for new beginnings. We found the power to rebuild and reimagine our town and our way of life for ourselves and our community. That power rested in the hands of the women.

We dedicated two years to helping our local community to

get back on its feet and then decided to think bigger.

I'd started a business from home a few years before. A fashion business designing bikinis. They were gorgeous, hand beaded, featuring bright colours and fabrics and they looked incredible on! But unfortunately, my inexperience in both fashion and business, my isolation and the distance from the city, my lack of mentors and peer support and zero industry connections meant that this business was sadly destined to fail.

My first business failed. But I now know that it was the key to my eventual success.

I thought about all the reasons my business had failed. A lack of support and professional development were the two major reasons things had gone wrong.

I needed to find a supportive community and access to learning, it all had to happen at flexible times and online as with three young children it was too hard to get to networking events or conferences. I did some searching online and found that there were a lot of other women just like me, who'd started businesses to enable them to be at home with their babies. We weren't like other business owners; we had all the challenges they faced plus a lot more! If I was ambitious but struggling, had great ideas but no one to turn to, had big dreams but felt alone in fulfilling them, what about the women all over Australia who felt isolated and needed support too? The more I talked to these women the more I realised we needed a dedicated online space where we could network, learn, share advice and support.

My sister had previously tried and failed to start a business too. So we teamed up, put our ideas together and came up with a vision to help women everywhere.

A place where you would always feel welcome, supported and included.

A place where you could share your challenges and your wins.

A place where you could find the connections that would be

pivotal to your business journey, if you needed an accountant, a graphic designer, the contact for the buying agent at Walmart or Harrod's, or to anyone at all, someone would know someone who could help you.

That's how it all began and today we have an incredible community of women surrounding us. Ambitious, determined, funny, generous and heart centred women who believe that they have the power to create their own lives and build a better world through their work.

We believe investing in women is the most powerful way to change the world. Women are running businesses that make a difference to the environment, people's lives, health, education, the planet or socially. I believe if we can help those women get their ideas up and going then we can really make huge changes in the world. It could cause a ripple effect that went on to create real change at a global level.

Can you imagine a world where everyone worked towards making the world a better place?

Where every business owner intentionally wrote their strategy for giving back and making a difference in their business plan.

A world where individuals encouraged and supported each other to make small changes in their daily lives, collectively to create a bigger impact.

A world where governments invest more in health and education than on military expenses.

Imagine a world where everyone played their part, shared their gifts and did what they could, where they were, with what they had, to make the world a better place.

I knew the impact on the world would be profound. This is our vision. To create a world where women step into their magnificence as leaders, where women's ideas are backed and given the support they need to really take off and a world where women and men work together to create a better future for us all.

My friend told me I couldn't change the world, but you know what, I already am and I'm going to keep going.

BIO:

Peace Mitchell is the CEO and co-founder of The Women's Business School, AusMumpreneur and Women Changing the World Press. She is the Australian Ambassador of Women in Tech and the Chair of global non profit - Tererai Trent International. Peace is also an international keynote speaker, TEDx speaker, best-selling author of Back Yourself, Courage and Confidence, The Women Changing the World, Goodbye Busy, Hello Happy, and Sacred Promise and host of The Best & Brightest podcast.

Peace Mitchell together with her business partner Katy Garner, co-founded AusMumpreneur in 2009 creating Australia's #1 community for mums in business and home of the national AusMumpreneur Awards. In 2016 they co-founded The Women's Business School to provide entrepreneurial education for women globally and in 2021 launched their publishing imprint Women Changing the World Press. They now have a community of over 150,000 women in business from around the world.

Peace is passionate about supporting women to reach their full potential. She has helped thousands of women achieve their dream of running a successful and profitable business. Peace received the Thought Leadership Award at the Stevie Awards in 2022, Diversity in Tech Mentorship Award in 2021 and the PauseFest SuperConnector Award in 2020.

www.thewomensbusinessschool.com

10
GLASS HOUSES

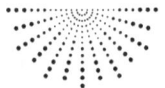

Kelly Biggs

Why would anyone want to read about me? Those are the thoughts that pop into my head while writing my chapter. I've squashed them down because I believe we all have a story to tell and although we're all individual and on different journeys, my experiences may help someone out there.

At school, I had no idea what I wanted to be when I grew up. This theme continued throughout my life. I felt less than. Everyone else knew what they wanted to do or were happy in jobs/careers/general life. Meanwhile I drifted in and out of jobs, never staying more than a few years.

I had been waiting all my life for something to take my interest, for my purpose, to just KNOW what I wanted to do. I didn't think that time would ever come.

I've always been creative and needed an outlet for it. From when I was a little girl, making weird and wonderful things out of toilet rolls, to my teenage years when my school books were full of doodles (which I often got told off for!).

Over the adult years I've had small side hustles; mobile phone accessories (back in the day when you could swap most parts out), personalised keyrings, box frames, keepsakes, jewellery and home décor but none of it was really my "thing". It felt good to make some money and have a creative outlet, but my interest always waned. I would hyperfocus for months at a time and then suddenly just let everything slide.

During a creative slump in 2015, I went on a weekend glass fusing course as something new to try. I had no idea what glass fusing even was! On that course I finally had my WOW moment. I enjoyed it so much, it felt like a passion had ignited within me. I decided there and then that THIS is what I wanted to do. And so, I did. At the time I was working long hours in a supermarket, but I was away from my young son a lot and rarely saw my partner. I hated the job and was miserable. I took every overtime opportunity and saved up enough money to buy a kiln, tools, glass, and everything else. People said I was mad; I couldn't possibly set up a business based on one basic course. I'm so glad I didn't listen.

I have lots of people in my life who don't know about my past. I don't tend to share my story, mostly because it feels a bit uncomfortable and could be viewed as a "sob story" but it isn't that, it's more a tale of perseverance, hard work and resilience.

Between 2007-2008, when I was 25, I made some bad decisions and ended up homeless and penniless. In a nutshell it was the worst time of my life. I was at rock-bottom and felt I had no way out. I lived in a homeless hostel which was not fit for human habitation, let alone the babies and children living there. 2 years later I managed to get a Housing Association flat, which again, despite the high rent charged, was another awful place. Don't get me wrong, I was so thankful for a roof over my head, but the conditions were terrible and did not help my mental health at the time. I felt like a loser and not worthy of anything.

During this time my dad died of Multiple Myeloma aged just 47, I was devastated. Watching him become more ill and frailer through the intensive treatments was heart wrenching. Throughout this time, I was full of self-doubt, in poverty, had debts, was taken to court because of a council benefit fault, did some questionable things which I still carry with me and felt huge judgement from myself and others. It was a difficult path, but I trod it and thankfully ended up coming out the other side. Losing my dad made me sit up and sort my life out.

Meeting my now partner changed a lot for me, and I'll always be thankful to him for lifting me up and making me realise I was worth something as a person, in my own right. I fell pregnant only 7 months into our relationship and although a baby wasn't meant to be on the cards for a while, we embraced the news and were excited to be a family. Unfortunately, it was a rocky time globally and he was made redundant. He secured an agency job and went on to be made permanent. But again, redundancy happened. All in, he was made redundant three times, and, on each occasion, it was scary and tested our limits.

All those things that happened have made me resilient. If I hadn't gone through that (and please realise, it would take a whole book to tell the full story) I certainly wouldn't be who I am today.

Back to business. Once I'd been running my business in the evenings for 2 years, I was in the position where I could cut my day job hours down to focus my attention on glass. I was still loving it. As time went on, it was getting harder to keep up with everything, so I made the huge decision to resign from the day job. I felt so courageous! I handed in my resignation and just a short time later discovered I was pregnant. The baby was very much longed for after lots of heartbreak, but I was still full of worry for my business, the family dynamic changing, the age gap between my children, how would my autistic son cope? How would I cope?

My first pregnancy was difficult and full of medical complications, and it happened again with my second baby but at the end of it I had a beautiful, healthy boy. I took 9 months off from my business, which was full of challenges and worries, but I enjoyed the time with my eldest son and the new baby, after I'd gotten through the awful post-natal depression.

I got back to work, and all my fears were unfounded. I still had customers! I doubt myself a lot, I have a fear of suddenly losing everything and I'd worked SO hard to build my business, learn new techniques and hone my skills but that fear was always with me. So, it was a beautiful surprise when I returned to work and found that people hadn't forgotten me!

I've been running my business 7 years now and I have learned so much about myself. In that time my son has been diagnosed autistic and ADHD and I am also on the waiting list for assessment as having gone through the process with him, it was glaringly obvious I am not neurotypical. Being neurodivergent comes with its own set of challenges but the beauty of being self-employed is that I can work around it. I can cut myself some slack if I'm having an off day. I can work to my own deadlines and reshuffle things, put processes in place to help me function within my business. I organise myself enough to overcome the executive dysfunction, the awful RSD (Rejection Sensitive Dysphoria) I experience and still make a success of my business.

But what is success? Of course, it's different for everyone. For me? It is earning money doing something I love while still being there for my children, supporting them and spending time with them. Having a passion, learning every day, and earning money from it feels like success, to me.

Since starting my business, I feel like I've been bombarded with advice, courses and mentors. Lots of people telling me what I should and shouldn't be doing. I got so overwhelmed with it all! I made some poor decisions because I didn't know what I was doing, and I didn't trust myself enough to be able to filter the advice. It was always well meant but as I became more established and learned more about myself and the way I work, I realised I just don't do things the same as others and that's okay! Many of the courses I did, some of the advice I was taking and lots of the things I paid for just weren't the right fit for me or my business. Now I know my business inside out and I know myself even better, I can filter out the "noise", the false promises, the disingenuous people who pretend they care, only to disappear when you no longer need their services.

I've mostly overcome the inferiority complex I carried around for years and the imposter syndrome, though they do still sometimes raise their heads! I now feel comfortable calling myself an artist. When I first started out, I absolutely hated calling myself that. It felt wrong. I had no qualifications in art, no formal learning, just a creative outlet in the form of glass. Who was I to call myself an artist? And those self-limiting beliefs were backed up by others in the glass world. There are many people who think you can't call yourself an artist (especially within glass) if you haven't done an exhibition, or if you've not had formal training or haven't been doing glass for 20+ years. It's all pretentious bullshit. I learned not to listen to those people.

It's always a good exercise to sit back and take stock, review how far you've come. I'm proud of my business, I've won two awards, one being Theo Paphitis SBS which is very dear to me. I have hundreds of 5-star reviews across different selling platforms. For someone who feels like I wing it every day, that's pretty good going. If I'm ever having a bad day full of doubt, I go and read the reviews my wonderful customers have left me.

If I've learned anything, it's that you must adapt, personally and within business. I absolutely hate change (unless I'm in control) and the fear of the unknown, but the pandemic taught me that adapting is always a good thing! I've added new ranges to my product offering which has enabled my business to grow, I've revisited my pricing and now ensure I get a fair wage for the work I do; I've rebranded and now reach many more customers than I did before. I ignore what others in my field are doing. Often it feels like a race to the bottom, everyone trying to undercut everyone else because of the misguided notion that people want everything cheap. It depends on what you're selling and who you're selling it to! But knowing your worth and your market is important. When I raised my prices, I actually got MORE sales. It is really tempting to lower prices or do discounts during a quiet spell; I've been there so many times. But once you start along that path, the only way is down.

My business is the longest thing I've stuck at. I absolutely love what I do. It is the hardest job I've ever had but it's also the most rewarding. I work long hours, but it enables me to be there for my children and support my family. I'm incredibly privileged to be in this position but it hasn't come about through luck. I made it happen. I have worked damn hard, persevered through some really tough times and I am still here, still doing what I love to do.

I had a dream and I made it work. Is my life perfect? Not by a long shot. But no-one's is. There are still things I need to work on, improve - within myself and my business.

Am I rich? No. But I'm not homeless. I have a roof over my head, food in my belly and so much love within my family. Being self-employed means some months are much tougher than others but generally, we get by.

I don't know what the future holds for me or my business but I'm still learning, enjoying and passionate about what I do. And that feels like a wonderful place to be.

BIO:

Kelly creates colourful, beautiful, functional, and decorative Fused Glass art, ashes keepsakes and DIY kits.

Kelly has worked hard over the years to offer beautiful handmade products, in original designs and offers amazing customer service.

She appreciates every order she gets, takes pride in her work, and creates the highest quality pieces for you to love and cherish.

www.vividluxglass.co.uk

11
MY MUSICAL HEART

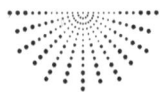

Becky Stevens

When I was 8, my two big sisters were playing in our local youth orchestra, and I went along to a concert with my parents. My mum asked me what instrument I wanted to play – the harp. They didn't have one in the orchestra, so I saw a gap to fill, and it sounded like a fun instrument to play, and a big instrument. My mum said no, it had to be an instrument I could see. So, I looked around. My sisters played flute and violin – that was winds and strings covered. I wanted to play the loudest instrument – the trumpet. There was a bit of debate due to me being heavily asthmatic, but eventually it was agreed.

Being a child who was heavily asthmatic wasn't fun. I'd struggle at sports – even though I loved it. When it snowed, my sisters would go out and play, and I'd go with them even when we all knew I hated it as I'd struggle breathing, get cold and start going blue. Every winter I'd have chest infections, be on antibiotics and steroids, go to hospital and be unable to play the trumpet for weeks on end.

But undeterred, I started playing and found I could do it, and was better than people thought I would be. My trumpet teacher spent a lot of time encouraging me to use my diaphragm to increase my lung capacity, sitting correctly to gain maximum fullness of the lungs and learning how to take effective deep breaths. To this day when asked to take a deep breath I'm always told "not that deep – maybe just a shallow breath will do!

As I got older, I ventured further with my trumpet playing. I was in various orchestras and bands and toured around Europe with them. I got accepted to a prestigious music course for my A levels, but I struggled with the management, and they quite often tried to get rid of me and failed. They took away my dream of being a trumpet teacher, and when the time came to decide my future path, my teenage self walked away from music and ventured into the world of work – retail.

I look back now at that child and realise that although I'm disappointed with that decision – I still believe it was the right one for me then.

I ventured into the world of work with one aim – to pay for me to do some travelling. I had already visited my sister in Mali, West Africa, when I was 17 and wanted to see more of the world. I went to Singapore and swam with dolphins. I went to New Zealand and did a bungee jump and got a tattoo. I went to Phoenix, Arizona and flew a Cessna by the Grand Canyon (and visited it too). I continued my gallivanting and working, having fun, and living my late teens and early 20s to the full.

I then had a car accident that caused a neck injury that looked like a possible shift of bones. An MRI showed that it was just damaged muscle which needed lots of physio and treatments to settle. The MRI also showed a grey area on the top of my right lung, which they thought could be a cyst. The report advised that cysts come and go and not to worry about it but suggested a visit to my GP to get it looked at. I was 21 and about to move from my family home in Sussex to Leicester. So, my GP suggested waiting until I settled in at Leicester to get it checked out – which I did, which resulted in me having a CT scan.

Then I got a letter from Glenfield Hospital, that turned my world upside down.

It wasn't from the lung department I had the scan with, but the heart department – inviting me to an appointment and to have an echocardiogram, ECG, and blood tests.

I was 21. I instantly phoned my mum.

All grown up, but still needed Mum

Having my mum come to the appointment was everything. She knew the language of doctors – especially heart ones. She knew, out of my siblings, I am not the emotionally strong one. I wear my heart on my sleeve and struggle with containing my emotions (whether happy or sad, angry or confused – there is always an element of tears!). She knew I would need her.

What I didn't know is that she knew more than me as to what was about to happen.

We turned up at Glenfield hospital, and as we got out of the car, she reached into the back and grabbed an envelope. I asked her what it was, and she replied that I only needed to know if it was relevant. My mind was already racing, talk about making it race more! We sat down in front of my cardiologist, and he started to explain what they had discovered.

My right lung was not connected to my heart properly and was causing the blood to flow to the wrong side of my heart. My right lung was not inflated and hadn't been since birth, so it wasn't producing oxygenated blood. And my heart was engorged on one side. This caused the heart to look like it had a line down the middle of it – like a Scimitar sword.

I had been born with Scimitar syndrome.

I should never have reached adulthood without it being picked up.

I had 70% oxygen supply in my blood.

I could have dropped dead at any time.

If not repaired, I would be blue by the time I was 40 due to lack of oxygen in my blood.

As my world collapsed, my mum stepped in with her envelope. She handed it to the doctor and asked him to explain the letter inside.

The letter was from Brighton hospital, where I had been born, dated nine weeks after I was born, stating I was a perfectly healthy baby and there was nothing wrong with my heart.

I was floored!! I knew the story of my birth – I was born blue and my dad wondered if I was his as I looked like an alien. But what I didn't know was that at birth they had done all sorts of tests, as they thought all my organs were back to front, and one junior doctor suggested I might have a heart problem. After a scan, which was new then, and x-rays the Consultant sent the letter, saying I was fine, and there was no doubt my heart and lungs would get stronger as I grew older. My mum had kept that letter, never knowing if she'd ever need it.

The Consultant informed us that in 1980 they didn't have the medical science to understand the condition. Now 20 years on, they see lots of babies with this condition as it's picked up early in the womb, and in some young children that have slipped through the net – but they hadn't seen it in an adult.

He explained that when you hear in the news of children or young adults dying suddenly on the games field, it was usually because of an undiagnosed congenital heart disorder. Most people with my undiagnosed condition don't reach adulthood.

I would need to have major heart surgery as soon as possible, with lots of tests and procedures to decide on what they wanted to do in the surgery. I left that room and collapsed. My world had just been shattered. I was 21 at the time and had just been told I had a heart birth defect that needed to be corrected straight away.

I was so nervous getting ready for surgery, but my GUCH nurse came and sat with me and my mum, keeping our spirits up and trying to calm my nerves.

This would be the last time I would see my chest scar free. 22 with a massive scar down my chest. I wasn't in a great place mentally and was struggling to deal with it.

I can't really remember going down for surgery – but I can remember coming round!

"Can you cough for me?" was the first thing I remember. Then the tube being removed from my throat – with a lot of coughing.

As my eyes flicked open, I realised I was surrounded by machines flashing, beeping, and printing. As well as about 4/5 nurses.

I don't think I was too panicked – all I wanted was water! My throat was so dry.

At some point, my mum came into the ICU and sat with me, letting me have ice chips to help with my throat. I was worried though and didn't want to scare the doctors and nurses, so I mentioned my worries to my mum.

"Mum, I think something's going wrong. I've got these red blotches on the palms of my hands".

Mum looked and smiled and let out a laugh. "That's perfectly normal – for the rest of us!"

See, my hands were usually just white. They hadn't had lots of oxygenated blood running through them before, and suddenly, I had pigment in my hands. And I now blush!! Something I still can't get over.

My oxygen levels had gone from 70% to 101%. I was now superhuman.

There have been many times since my surgery that I've been reminded of my surgery and how fragile life actually can be.
To think that I learnt to play the trumpet with one working lung without anyone realising it is a testament to my teacher and her teaching skills and to my parents who encouraged me to practice every day and not give in.

As a music teacher now, I am often challenged by my pupils who say, 'I haven't got enough puff, I'm not as big as you'. No matter your size, no matter your puff, perseverance will conquer. I'm living proof.

I'm a creative. I walk my own path, and I carry on even if things are against me. My life experience has taught me this, and through my business I am able to express myself in so many ways.

I'm a magpie for shiny silver things, and I create my own silver jewellery. I get inspired by random things I see, textures, ideas and love getting commissions from people who see my work.

I'm a chocolate lover, and my chocolate obsession has grown over the years. I discovered a way to make chocolate-based fudge using a slow cooker and became hooked on becoming Willy Wonka. I love creating new flavours and designs.

Throughout everything I've been through, music has been at the heart of it. If I'm not playing it, I'm listening to it or humming away in my head.

And from offering help at a village school, conducting their school band, I've developed a passion for sharing music with others.

I now teach all brass instruments in schools, online and at home in my purpose-built studio.

Silver Beats and Treats, my business, brings all my 3 loves and passions together.

It may be quirky that those 3 different things make up a business, but the way I see it is:

- Why should we focus on one thing, when we enjoy doing lots of different things?
- Why should we fit in with the normal that we're expected to?

My whole life has been a series of ups and downs, but my passions have always been there.

So, I focus on them.

BIO:

Becky Stevens is the owner of Silver Beats and Treats. She makes handmade silver jewellery and is the creator of beginner silver clay home kits. Becky teaches beginner piano and brass locally, online nationally, and online internationally. She also creates fabulous chocolate-based fudge for treats and occasions.

Becky is also walking 20 walks of 20 miles, raising awareness for The Somerville Heart Foundation – 20 years after her surgery.

www.silverbeatsandtreats.com

12
BEING ALIVE. IT'S EVERYTHING.

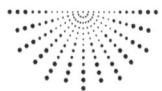

Kelly Bentley

Have you ever lain down under the stars and thought about the expanse of the universe? Sounds out there, I know, but if you haven't done it yet, give it a try. It makes one feel insignificant - perhaps overwhelmed - by the sheer size of it. The opposite is true for when you think about living in the moment or understanding the value of time. If you really think about, and better still, live these two statements, you realise the insignificance of everything else and paradoxically, realise the significance of you. It is something we should all do. Sadly, most of us do it too late like when we've lost a loved one, suffered a health scare or even lost some part of ourselves to regret.

I never thought I had a story to tell. Maybe I still don't, but my journey has also taught me the power of impacting just one person. Just. One. Person.

So here I go in the hope that I engage authentically with you. The reality is this chapter is for you as much as it is for me. For humans to engage and grow meaningfully, we need to bare our souls, share our experiences and look for the commonality in the communities around us.

That said, I'm not one to share every meal or every time my dog looks cute - no judgement - my love for social media and its ridiculous brainwashing vortex is waning! But every now and then even a blind squirrel finds an acorn and then I am moved or influenced positively to do better or keep trying.

So, I hope this piece helps at least one person believe in their journey, to not lose hope when it seems that is all there is left to do, to carry on loving life in each moment, good or bad, to show compassion and understanding both for yourself and those you know and do not know and mostly to be curious and open rather than judgmental and fatalistic about the world we live in.

In August 2019, some of the most influential years of my life began. I decided to go back to being an entrepreneur at 35. I had once owned my own business, but it hadn't gone the way I wanted – a great learning curve, steep but necessary. Three days after I resigned, my mum was admitted to hospital, she had a double cancer; two primary instances of different cancers – super rare and completely misunderstood by her medical team.

My plans to start my business were replaced with 12-hour days at the hospital for the next 12 weeks. A month after that, she died in my arms at 10.07am at the tender age of 57 leaving behind three children still under the age of 18. A week later, we had to put our beloved French Bulldog, Harvey, down. Four weeks after that my grandfather passed away and I got malaria from my mum's memorial in Zambia and was hospitalised for a week. Two weeks after that we went into a Level 5 lockdown in South Africa because of COVID-19.

All hopes of my events business starting were dashed. And so, the rollercoaster of self-doubt began. I had resigned eight months earlier and my business hadn't even gotten off the ground. My savings were running out and now COVID meant we couldn't earn. Four months later, deep into the uncertainty of lockdown cycles we've all come to know so well, and nine months after my mum passed away, I, too, was diagnosed with cancer.

Enough with the war stories. Suffice to say that it was a sh*t 12 months. Life, apparently, had been saving up a whole lot of curveballs and threw them my way all at once with very little time in-between.

Why am I telling you all this?

Well, this is where the doubt came in about whether or not it would be valuable to you as the reader. I do think it's always necessary to give context. Sharing experiences helps with connection. It opens people's eyes to what is out there. Sometimes, it comforts people to know they are in a similar boat. Whatever your specific reason is, my intention for telling you my story is to highlight one thing. You are alive.

Sounds silly but most of us take it for granted. Also, to share the good that came out of everything I have gone through; an acorn which hopefully encourages you to keep going, dig deeper, not give up. I'm certainly not out of the woods yet. But I now know and understand that each day is worth my undivided attention.

The last two years bringing me to August 2022 have been nothing short of chaotic, up and down, in and out. They have tested my faith, my relationships, my work ethic and my self-belief. They have also opened my eyes. I was told three times my cancer was worse than previously thought. That in fact, it was due to negligence that it hadn't been picked up and everything could have been avoided. I had to undergo IVF treatment to extract my eggs and only had three weeks to do it. My husband and I needed to do this because we weren't sure how invasive the cancer was with partial Lymphovascular invasion adding to the complexity. Good news though. I did go on to have two intensive IVF rounds in three weeks following my diagnosis and was blessed beyond measure with successful extraction.

I then underwent one of the first surgeries of its kind in South Africa with four surgeons, six hours of surgery and 10 days of ICU care. I came out of the hospital a changed human in more ways than I understood at the time. Since my surgery at the end of 2020, I've had to find my way with very limited medical understanding of my case in South Africa and the resulting complications, I've had to have another surgery, bid farewell to falling pregnant naturally, be forced into premature menopause, flooded with hormones because mine never really recovered from the aggressive IVF process, experience a failed attempt to transfer and then nearly have the second attempt highjacked by the finding of a benign liver tumour.

BUT the point is this…I am alive.

What I did in-between was eventually start my business on 1 July 2020. It wasn't pretty, and it didn't have the clarity it needed to be valuable to my target market. Like so many businesses, I needed to pivot. In-person experiences weren't an option and my passion was in making a sustainable impact through connection and relationships. Back to the drawing board I went. There were a few things needed – expertise outside of my own, a clearly articulated value proposition geared towards a new economic reality, reaching out of my comfort zone, facing deep-seated fears and relinquishing control. As a Type A, this list was rather daunting. I have addressed a few things but it's an ongoing exercise of looking in the mirror and conversing with my ego… There are good days and bad days.

However, I am immensely proud that The Rebel Element was born and flourished in its 18 months of existence as a stakeholder engagement consultancy. I was joined by a dear friend who helped shape and adapt our new go-to market approach. Following a speaking engagement at the end of 2021 and long-term relationship with a 15-year-old B2B tech marketing agency in Kenya, we decided to join forces to drive digital transformation across the African continent. In April 2022, our two businesses merged to become dx[5]. A 30-person strong agency with an expansive and valuable network for which I have the honour and privilege of leading as Group CEO. I've faced my ego daily; I'm becoming more aware of the role it plays in my actions. Sometimes, it is disappointing. Other times, pleasantly surprising.

We have also just undergone our first successful IVF transfer. We pray for a successful outcome. Even if God's plan is different for us, I know that it is a miracle that we have gotten to this point. I can't be more grateful for the highs and the lows.

Someone once said to me, 'you shouldn't tell your story while you're in the middle of it. It's too hard. Too emotional'. Well, I politely disagree. Our stories are a continuum made up of every experience, every action, every normal day and every chaotic day, every joy and every trauma. If you cry when you tell your story, that's ok. If you laugh, that's ok too. Our stories **ARE** who we are. And every day, good or bad, we get to continue them because we are alive. So, next time you meet someone new, ask them to tell you their story, encourage them, listen and appreciate their journey and maybe, just maybe, because you took the time, something will surprise you and impact your own journey.

What have I learned?

That list is too long, and this chapter has a word count, but here it is. The key things that have applied to me personally and professionally:

1. You are alive – don't take it for granted.
2. Clarity is kindness.

3. Always assume the best in other people – they may let you down, but you haven't taken on the poison of negative assumption before that point.
4. The wrong decision is better than no decision.
5. Don't accept mediocrity from yourself or others.
6. Acknowledge when you have played a role in disabling someone.
7. Kaizen – 1% continuous improvement everyday amounts to a lifetime of achievement.
8. Put your pride aside and ask for help - it's not weak. It demonstrates courage.
9. Accountability works both ways.
10. Learn and action the power of 'no, thank you,'. Being a people pleaser drains your energy.
11. Sharpen your focus. Cut back, a jack of all trades and master of none is not valuable to anyone least of all yourself.
12. Ego. get to know yours. It is either your Achilles heel or greatest asset.
13. Actively listen. The most valuable information is often found in the seemingly unimportant conversations both with yourself and with others.
14. You have to be helpable. Don't underestimate the impact you have on whether other people support you or not.
15. Sorry doesn't work with the word 'but'
16. Be a nice human. Prioritise having fun. We are not here for long so do everything you can to leave a 'smile legacy.'

BIO:

Kelly Bentley is well, Kelly. She shows up. And when she does you will know; rebelling without a pause to humanise B2B engagements. Co-Founder & CEO of dx^5 she has been at the forefront of, and championing, business optimisation and stakeholder engagement across the African continent. With a sales and marketing leadership background in the technology industry working across the USA, Europe and Africa for over 20 years.

Kelly brings people together as a connector – building communities around their unique needs leveraging skill, experience, and influence to drive value and help people make better business decisions. A marketeer as per dictionary.com but in reality, a relationship artist. Kelly creates engagement opportunities to help buy or sell digital solutions by understanding the demand, and building effective associations.

Passionate about authentic connection and pan-African growth with a focus on partnerships and the unique dx^5 human-centric engagement model, Kelly acts on, and gets results with ease thanks to her credibility and level of trust in and from her network. When Kelly asks, or makes an introduction, her network carries weight, and inspires people to respond.

www.rebelwithoutapause.me

13
FALL DOWN SEVEN, GET UP EIGHT LADY!

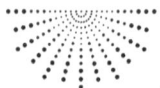

Kylie Patchett

When I was a little girl I was convinced that when I grew up, I would a) be the boss of something and b) be a raging success. Back then, success meant getting a "good job" with "good money", a lot of responsibility and (weirdly) wearing high heels. But at the age of 26 when I found myself a GM of a private medical company and climbing the corporate ladder, I learnt that particular version of success didn't actually float my boat.

As I have grown older and wiser, it has dawned on me that there were several things I got wrong with this ill-fitting perception of success, and that these same mistakes can lead us astray in any area of life - relationships, finances, self worth, career, even parenting.

Once I learnt to reject and reframe these unwritten rules, and started leaning into their flip side, I've been on a journey of what I like to call consciously creating the life I crave. The biggest point of learning for me was that my belly and body always know, and my sense of fulfilment and joy are directly correlated to how closely aligned to my core values I am living.

My first foray into entrepreneurship grew out of the utter devastation of losing my father, and reinventing myself as a health coach - something that combined all western medical science background with my deep dive into Eastern medicine and health coaching study. Man oh man, did I love the high of coaching other women, and seeing firsthand their results when they put their own needs first. My health coaching program Destination Delicious still stands as one of my career highlights, with the friendships and connections formed in this group still standing almost a decade later for some of the ladies.

So life was good ... until it wasn't.

With the gift of hindsight, I can clearly see I allowed myself to get pulled off track. I bought into other people's rules (5 figure months, multiple 6 figure years, 90 day marketing plans anyone?) and listened to business coaches who said you could never make good money unless you were coaching other coaches.

So rather than staying in my own soul-satisfying lane, I regrettably turned my hand to business coaching. With a professional background in business strategy, leadership coaching and marcomms, I was well within my wheelhouse but I ignored my inner compass at my own peril. Yes, my business coaching courses were successful to a degree, but I was missing one of my personal keys to success - alignment to my own values and my own joy.

Fast forward 2 more years and I had gotten so out of alignment, I ended up creating just another "work hard to make money" j-o-b for myself, and not the soul satisfying, sustainable business I originally signed up for.

So I took a leap of faith, burned my business to the ground and walked away - returning to corporate for another five years. Those five years also saw a move to the country, our girls turning into teens, someone close suffering a serious accident and a whole lot of forced healing around childhood trauma and addiction.

You'd think that would be the end of my entrepreneurial journey, but my heart had other ideas. Earlier this year I received a deep and clear message in my morning meditation - "it's time to share the next level of what you have learnt and lived through".

To say I was reticent is an understatement. "I don't want to put myself out there again, to start all over again, to make the same mistakes", I whinged.

But the heart knows what the heart wants, and this feeling wouldn't let me be. So here I am. On a chilly Southern Hemisphere evening, writing to you and sharing this oddly stretching and satisfying journey.

This iteration of entrepreneurship, I started very differently to my first. My first was all about strategy, sales and trying to figure out the perfect pitch. Of trusting other people's advice above my own. Of making some pretty darn big mistakes. And yes, a degree of success.

This time around, my heart desires simple, slow, soulful and aligned. I can move very fast and turn an idea into reality in a short timeframe. But I realise this is part of my issue - last time I got caught by my own speed. I forgot to check in, to take a breath and acclimatise, to ask my sweet soul if we were on the right track, to settle into what I truly desire.

And that, my love, is time and spaciousness to en-joy my life, to create my own art, to build something special that I can feel and see, to spend time with my family, to go riding motorbikes in big-sky country back roads on a perfect Wednesday afternoon with my love.

To work with women who want more to life than just the grind of doing-all-the-things-because-that's-what-the-rules-are, of the juggle of home life, daughtering, wifeing, mothering, working and all the other hats we've been taught we need to wear to be a good girl.

To coach and build community where women have a soft place to land, a self healing haven to embrace the time of midlife when we may finally have the space, time and resources to actually take a beat and ask "what the heck do I really want" "who am I?" "What is my purpose here?".

To experience the goosebumps of those a-ha moments, those chiropractic adjustments of the soul when a woman steps into who she is way down deep in the core of her being, who unapologetically stakes her claim on what she really wants, who invests time and attention into her own healing, and by doing so lights the way for others to do the same.

To embody all that I share, to actually take my own damn advice, to stretch into self connection, to take the time for daily devotions to my own health and wellbeing, and to continue to unlearn the limitations and trauma responses I learnt in a codependent childhood.

And this time I am not willing to settle for anything less.

So how can I help you, in your business and life's journey? Perhaps sharing the pitfalls, or unwritten rules I was following which led me astray may help you to avoid the same mistakes.

In other words, this is my advice on how NOT to create a life and business that feels nourishing - mind, body and soul. Even though it may be comfortable, familiar and safe to follow these unwritten rules; my big, bold and very beautiful invitation is to lean into a completely different way of being.

Playing by someone else's rules - Assuming someone else's version of success is the same thing that will fulfil you. No one else knows you, truly knows you and all that you need, want and desire. Trust your own instincts. If something doesn't feel good, don't force it. If it's not a hell yes, it's a no or at least a no right now.

Ignoring your inner compass - Letting the head rule without also checking on the wisdom of the body and soul, and sticking and staying even though you have that gut feel that something isn't right. We've been taught to be logical and think our way into and out of everything in life. But your soul knows your path.

Believing your brain BS - The very last thing you want to do, considering your brain is literally wired to keep you safe (and therefore potentially playing small). Your brain filters for threats and what you expect to see. If you have been imprinted as a kid to expect drama or lack or abuse, your brain literally filters for things that match that reality. Your brain is an absolute gem at keeping you alive, but it may not be wired to align to what you want to create (yet!), so beware.

Denying your deepest desires - Neglecting the most important relationship there ever will be (hello self trust!). Please stop lying to yourself, diluting what you desire, or trying to play a role which is not you. You are here for a reason, your deepest, truest desires are here for a reason too. Keeping yourself smaller than you are called to be ain't serving anyone. The end.

Going for good enough - Continuing on a trajectory of meh, because you just don't believe deep joy, true freedom, whatever your highest values are, are actually available to you. I cannot say this loud enough. "Good enough" is a form of self neglect. How do you really want to feel when you wake up, when you look into a lover's eyes, when you show up for your career? Go chase THAT. Yes, you really can. Yes, you really deserve it.

Fearing failure so much you won't try - There really is no such thing as failure. Each time you try and something doesn't work out, you learn. You wouldn't chastise a little person for falling down when they learn to walk so why would you chastise yourself when you're learning a new skill? Fall down seven, get up eight Lady.

And a sneaky little side note for midlife mavens - particularly if starting or growing a business is part of something you have always wanted, but never quite given yourself permission to dive right in and all of a sudden that nudge is re-emerging in the space and grace of your mid years and beyond...

Sweet woman, I see you. Standing on the cusp of midlife, wondering if it's too late, too hard or too unreachable to create the life you truly crave; to give yourself permission to put down the weight of old limits, to unbind from the rules and obligations you've been sold, to surrender all that no longer truly, madly, deeply serves you.

But what if you're not on the threshold of a midlife crisis... not "over the hill", not "your best years are behind you", not "the change of life" and all the other negative connotations of peri-menopause and beyond.

What if it's not a midlife crisis...not a time of life to be feared, but a time to intentionally dive into the unknown with wild abandon and an open heart? A time ripe for reinvention, time to reflect and honour the hard-won lessons; to take stock. To reinvent, to begin to heal, to rewild yourself. Time to marinate in the sweet relief of having no one to please but you.

So, if starting or growing your own business is part of what you deeply desire, set your sails to the billowing breeze of your inner compass, let my hindsight be your foresight and keep checking in with that sweet soul of yours, for she knows the way to the life you crave.

> *"Success is not the key to happiness.*
> *Happiness is the key to success.*
> *If you love what you are doing, you will be successful"*
> Herman Cain

BIO:

A Msc Forensic Biologist, Kylie Patchett has spent the past 20+ years leading and mentoring in the scientific, health and wellbeing sectors and has recently returned to entrepreneurship as a Womens' Wellbeing Coach. She's a two time best-selling author, certified holistic health coach, NLP and EFT practitioner, Vinyasa yoga and Traditional Chinese Medicine trained, and Zen Thai shiatsu masseuse.

On a mission of self-healing since the age of 16, Kylie has transformed childhood trauma, binge eating and a deep lack-based scarcity mindset into living her best, most simple and spacious life in country Queensland, Australia with her teen daughters and firey husband.

Kylie is the founder of the The Radiance Revolution, a groundswell of women embracing midlife as a time of metamorphosis - a time ripe for reinvention, a time of life to be savoured and celebrated, its power claimed.

She believes healed women, heal the world, and that is very good news for all of us.

www.linktr.ee/kyliepatchett

14
NAVIGATING THROUGH LIFE'S STORMS

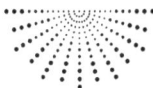

Ursula Stroh

The below is a note I wrote to myself in the Grange Tower Bridge Hotel, London on the last night before I joined a crew to sail around the world. I tucked the note into a little box together with an anchor charm to represent my return to terra firma after the circumnavigation. I left the little box in a bag to be only accessed again if I were to return safely after a year at sea.

"Be very, very proud! Congratulations! You are incredible and you deserve only the best that life has to offer! If you are reading this, you should know, you can do anything!!!!"

We left London on the 1st of September 2013. I remember how scared I was. How unfathomable the experience ahead seemed to be. How vulnerable I felt.

To explain how I got to this point and what made me want

to sail around the world, I want to share with you a snippet of my life story.

I completed my PhD in Change and Communication Management in 2004 with external examiners in the USA who then offered me a job in Maryland to teach at the top School in my field. I took the role and my husband at the time decided, a couple of months before we were both supposed to move there, to stay behind in Australia to complete his own studies. For a year we had a Skype relationship where we spoke every day.

Typical of high-achieving academic work, even after studying for several years in the field, I was so scared to be outed as an imposter. As a result, I worked myself to exhaustion every day, late hours, and weekends - research papers, preparing for lectures, presenting reports, grading, and supervising.

One day my husband mentioned on a call that Steve Irwin had died. I was in tears because I really respected what he did for Australian wildlife. I asked him how it happened. He mentioned that Steve died while working with stingrays. I stopped crying, feeling better and said to him that at least Steve died doing something that he was passionate about. He was surprised at my sudden change of emotions and said: "Wow, so does that mean that if I die in a paragliding accident, you would not be upset?"

I replied that I wouldn't really be upset. Of course, I would be sad, but much less upset than if he died of cancer, or a car accident, or something similar.

He then responded mockingly: "so, how are you going to die one day? Being hit by a book against your head?"

I was so shocked by this! Was that how he saw me? Was that how the world saw me? That my passion was just books and studying? What a boring way to die! What a boring life! I reflected intently on this, and it made me incredibly sad. I had worked so hard, for what? To be so ordinary? This haunted me and stayed in the back of my mind.

A few years later my marriage fell apart, which was not something I wanted or planned for myself. I was devastated by it. Together with that, my dad had cancer and was very ill. I couldn't be with my family, my job was very stressful and demanding, and I was exhausted! I just broke down. Completely. And I'm talking seriously suicidal.

But during this downward spiralling process, I saw a Facebook post with the words: 'You can break a woman down temporarily, but a real woman will always pick up the pieces, rebuild herself, and come back stronger than ever.' (Anonymous)

This talked to me. And I started thinking: How can I rebuild myself? How can I become stronger?

I felt I needed to get myself completely out of my comfort zone. I needed a challenge and a big change.

On the train on the way to work one day, in the middle of that turmoil, pain, and loneliness, surrounded by people squashed against me, I saw a sign next to the station at Waverton, Sydney that read: Clipper 13-14; 12 new yachts; 40,000 miles; 1 global race. It stipulated that no experience was required, and they were recruiting ordinary people for a challenge of their life. My heart was racing wildly.

I got off the train and applied as soon as I got into the office.

I had no sailing experience whatsoever. I grew up in Johannesburg, in the middle of South Africa, far from the sea and I had been on a sailing boat maybe three times in my life.

It was probably foolish ignorance to even think I could do it. It was a few months before my 50th birthday. I was divorced, sad, broken, had no money, and just wanted the hurt of everything that was happening to me to go away. And this is how I chose to do it.

So, I took up three part-time jobs, sold everything of value, put my few belongings in storage, my broker helped me to mortgage myself up, and I took a voluntary redundancy. It was financially the worst thing I could ever have done.

I was so clumsy on deck, and I knew nothing about sailing. I didn't speak 'boat'. I was almost dangerous as a crew mate. But I learnt, and was determined to be a good sailor. I tried so incredibly hard. And it was really, really hard. We were only four women on a boat of 20 crew. We were not treated any differently.

To connect back to my story of how I was going to die one day…

The Southern Ocean was the most remote and scariest place I have ever experienced. It was freezing cold with the wildest of weather.

We had the most severe hurricanes – over 115 knots of wind and seas you just can't forget. The noise of the wind was overwhelming with rain coming at us horizontally like needles in big drops. The sea, an angry mess that dumped large amounts of water all over you.

In the middle of one of these storms, I was on deck with four of my crew mates. We sat huddled together for warmth and to provide some support against the fear of this drama unfolding around us.

At some intense point, we had to lower the staysail and hoist the storm jib. We were obviously tethered on and battled for what felt like forever to get to the bow of the boat. I remember how the boat went through the waves. It nosedived through the water, and in those moments we were lifted from the deck, and the force of the water and wind made it difficult to breathe. And then, as we came out of the wave, we were smashed hard against the deck. We took our next breath as we saw the next wave coming, and I thought: Today I am going to die! This is it! I was so scared. The fear filled my body with such intensity that I was shaking all over and tears just poured down my face. This was life and death stuff and my life passed vividly through my mind. I can remember saying to myself: so, this is how it is going to happen. This is how I am going to die. In the middle of a storm in the Southern Ocean!

And then, in that terrifying chaos the Steve Irwin conversation came up and I thought: Oh wow! This is not a book against my head! This is the most incredible storm in the most incredible place on earth on a boat with my crew mates. What a most wonderful way to die!

And suddenly this storm was the most beautiful thing I had ever experienced. The air was crisp, and the sea was ferociously blue, and the drama was suddenly exhilarating, and the best adrenalin rush I have ever had. My fear turned to fascination and awe.

My story in my head, my attitude, my paradigm changed. The storm didn't change, but my life sails, my mindset sails were adjusted and trimmed.

A year later I finished the race with my crew. And I did that race with tenacity and perseverance. The woman I met in myself at the exact place she started the circumnavigation was a woman with no doubt of who she'd become. She had changed. Sunburnt eyes, sky blue weathered, but warrior brave through a fearless smile. She wore a quiet calm with confidence and acceptance of what life had dished out.

I'd almost forgotten about the note in my bag, but I still get goosebumps when I think of that moment I opened the little box. I did feel proud. And what I was most proud of, is not once in those 12 months did I break down. Not once did I lose it, throw a tantrum, or give up. I kept going. I kept turning up for the next leg and the next ocean crossing.

Sometimes I still don't know how I did it. It was the hardest thing I'd ever done. But it was also the most life-changing, most courageous, most challenging and best thing I'd ever done.

It set me on a path of constant change. Changes I've instigated, or big changes that have happened to me. To us all. That is what our lives are now. Constant change. We've recently experienced the pandemic that changed the world irrevocably. Think about the war in Ukraine, extreme environmental changes and world economic changes. And as we get older changes happen more often – like deaths and divorce and menopause and for some, children leaving home. Loss.

But I now realise that all these changes also opened doors and created opportunities that I never would've had. For example, I subsequently sailed from Tahiti to Sydney through the South Pacific for a year with a man I met on the race, which was the absolute highlight adventure of my life... so far!

Going through changes taught me to be stronger and more resilient. I think it helped me through the isolation of the pandemic, and related work and relationship changes.

It also brought about a realisation that I want to share my learnings, my insights, and my story with those who might be battling with ways to cope with changes in their lives. It gave me the courage to leave the corporate, salaried world of a secure job, and build my own business guiding people through change.

Change is tough and sometimes heart-wrenchingly lonely. With the right tools and support we can learn to respond to changes with a spirit of adventure and opportunity. Leaders and teams in organisations find this especially useful to cope with the new ways of working in a hybrid environment, a very different business environment, and a complete transformation in employee, client and customer expectations.

I find a great deal of satisfaction and meaning in my work when I see the transformation in my clients as they find their own inner strength, and face their fears with renewed confidence, calm and acceptance.

My business is still in its build-up phase and that, in itself, presents known and unknown challenges. But I am determined, just like every time I walked to the boat for a new leg of the race and tried to find any possible excuse not to go, to face my fears with courage and persistence – one step at a time.

And it can't be harder than sailing the Southern Ocean, right?

BIO:

Dr Ursula Stroh is an adventurer and sailor with a PhD in Change Management. In her business, Trim Your Sails, she works with individuals, leaders and teams to navigate through change by focusing on their values, strengths, resilience, and relationships.

www.facebook.com/trimyoursailschange

15

SO, WHAT NOW...?

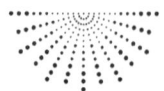

Kirsty Dorling

This is not a neat and tidy story about starting and growing a business. It's more a tale of realisation that being independent and away from a safe and predictable career is actually possible. Not only is it possible, it's wonderful! But my transition out of the ordinary and into the unknown was definitely not smooth. Six years ago, I left my teaching career of 16 years, and not in the way I thought I would.

I didn't *choose* to become a teacher. At the age of 21 after completing a degree in dance and drama I quickly caved into the pressure of 'getting a proper job'. My dream of acting professionally was just that, a dream. I swept it aside, not having the confidence to chase it. I got work teaching dance and acting in further education colleges. I met some great people - most of which, like me, were not really teachers at heart but were talented dancers, musicians, writers and artists. One chance meeting even led to a short spell of acting work with a tour of small theatres along the south coast, a play at the Brighton Festival and the year after, a short residency in a London pub theatre. It was wonderful, but it didn't pay the bills and so ultimately, teaching won. Here's something people don't often talk about, once you're a teacher - it's really hard to think you could do anything else.

So, despite not really being happy in my work life - my *real* life was great. Bought a flat at 22, married the love of my life at 24, baby at 26 another at 29, may as well have another one at 32. Ok, so what now? 4 house moves later and we'd kind of run out of life changing decisions.

I realised I'd been ignoring how miserable I was at work, I longed for Friday and dreaded Sunday night. But I just accepted it. I thought this was what life was and I felt totally trapped in my job. I squashed down my feelings of anxiety and low self-esteem and just got on with it, calm and collected on the outside - cracking and breaking more and more each day on the inside.

Then I finally broke.

In January 2016 after a pretty full-on emotional breakdown, I plunged into a dark and depressed world. Struggling to get out of bed and hounded by anxiety, one thing was certain, I had reached my limit. The five words my husband said to me at that time were the lifeline that I was clinging to, "you're not going back there". The problem was… if I wasn't going back to teaching, where was I going? What do I do now?

After two months of darkness, something unexpected pulled me out. I came across a YouTube video that *totally* changed my whole outlook on my future. A TED Talk by the wonderful Patti Dobrowolski entitled 'Draw Your Future' (go and watch this immediately - wait, hang on! Finish reading this first, it's about to get really good).

It turns out drawing your current situation and your desired future is powerful stuff - you don't have to be great at drawing, but you do have to be honest with yourself. Taking up

Dobrowolski's 'double dare' to her audience to draw that dream, that desired new reality, it suddenly began to feel tangible….and once that picture exists, it's hard to ignore. Reinforced by her mantra, "see it, believe it, act on it" I began to do exactly that.

I discovered a franchisee opportunity with a company called Pyjama Drama, a chance to build a business running children's drama and imaginative play sessions, delivering interactive performances and providing children's party entertainment. Now, the old me would have taken ages to even think about calling them up, my nerves and shyness would have gotten the better of me…but not anymore! I acted on it and took small steps everyday towards starting my own franchise business, which launched in June 2016.

Ok, so time to press the fast forward button…. here's 2016-2019 in a nutshell (an amazingly fulfilling, exciting and joyful nutshell, just for the record). I met hundreds of fantastic families and delivered thousands of Pyjama Drama sessions across Hampshire. My love of performing was renewed as I delivered parties for rooms full of excited children and had an amazing time entertaining them. I toured the roads of Southampton in my branded car arriving at nurseries and schools to be greeted by joyful squeals of "Pyjama Drama's here!" I turned up at charity events, carnivals, holiday clubs…I burst onto the Kids Stage at festivals having the time of my life performing and igniting little imaginations. Wherever there were kids, you can be sure I was there, singing, playing and leaping around on an imaginative adventure! I grew my business to a point that I was able to pay myself the same as I was earning in my old teaching job.

Life was good - no more Sunday blues, no more feeling undervalued, overlooked and excessively anxious. I had found my happy place and was enormously proud of my business. So why on earth would I want to change things? Why, as I'm

SHINE ON YOU CRAZY DAISY - VOLUME 6

writing this, am I looking for someone to buy my beloved Pyjama Drama business?

Well, hand in hand with running a business comes the world of social media - love it or hate it, if you run a business, it's the best way to reach new people and build a strong identity in the ever-growing online world. Turns out - I loved using social media and became fascinated with the creative side of each platform.

I was asked to deliver a social media talk at the Pyjama Drama annual seminar and after a throwaway comment from one of the directors, "I wish you could run the Head Office social media" I thought…. well, why can't I?

So, still inspired by my new mantra…. I acted on it and wrote a proposal for the Head Office involving me taking over the content creation and management of their social media channels. They said YES, and not only for the UK, but for the branch of Pyjama Drama in California too! So, while my own business was still thriving, I now had another focus and a new creative challenge.

Ok, that takes us to the end of 2019….so we all know what's coming and I'll be honest, I'm hovering on that fast forward button again - as really, wouldn't we all like to forget the 'C' word ever existed? But 2020 arrived and with it came lockdown….and with that, disaster for so many businesses across the world. But I was not going without a fight, and fight I did. Together with an amazing team of Pyjama Drama franchisees we built an online following. We discovered that it was possible to entertain, engage with and inspire children through the tiny cameras on our phones. Through eighteen months of confusion, tears, frustration, illness, financial hardship and sheer determination, we made it through. I still had a business on the other side of lockdown.

So, what now? Off I go again, straight back out there to find new customers and start again? The truth is the pandemic had taken its toll.... I'll admit I was a little broken, a bit lost and totally exhausted! Although I had a core of super loyal, amazing customers, time had moved on and ultimately, I needed to do some serious re-building to get my business back to what it was, and I just wasn't motivated.

But what I *was* motivated by was the social media work I was doing. So, what now? Could this actually be a business? Could I help and support other business owners to feel confident on social media? Ok, I knew what I had to do.... remember that mantra? "See it, believe it, act on it". So, I did. I started an Instagram page, I contacted business owners I knew and offered a free trial of my services, I took courses, I researched, I experimented with creating new types of content, I studied insights and created marketing strategies. Within the first three months I had three new clients, and I began to realise this *could* be a business (ok, forget that - this IS a business!) The Insta House was born, and it was mine.... ALL mine! So, what now? Time to build a website, sort out my branding, spread the word - this is it, I'm off on a new adventure - This is what I needed. THIS is what I need to do now!

So, while I don't think the pandemic ended my Pyjama Drama business, it certainly hurt it. But maybe Pyjama Drama had already done what it was always meant to do. It gave me joy when I thought all hope was lost, it built my confidence and helped me discover who I really am, it made me hugely proud and it opened the door to the world of social media, and to my next adventure.

The Insta House is, like any business, still evolving and changing. It's already leading to exciting opportunities (things that the old me would have been far too scared to take on). Now I jump at the chance to try something new, I thrive on working out how to do things on my own and I feel confident in my ability to provide valuable support and creative energy to a whole range of business owners.

When I look back to who I was six years ago, I just don't recognise myself. It's a cliche to say "I'm not that person anymore" but maybe that's not a cliche. If you're confident and assured enough to say a statement like that, and more importantly, if you've made steps forward towards a new life, then I reckon it's not a cliche.... it's freedom!

So, if you're not happy and you see an alternative, a glimmer of hope in the dark, take the chance, because if your heart is truly in it...it isn't actually a chance. It's YOUR future and it's waiting for YOU - it's happening now! So, what are you still doing here? Get going.... see it, believe it, act on it. I did, and I've loved every moment.

BIO:

Kirsty is an experienced educator, actor and business owner having taught dance and drama in Further Education for sixteen years and run Pyjama Drama, a successful drama and imaginative play business for children in Hampshire. She now runs The Insta House, a social media management company that specialises in helping small to medium sized businesses to create and grow an exciting online presence and get the best from their social media content. She lives with her husband Henry, three children Jay, Ewan and Alicia and Winnie the dog!

www.theinstahouse.com

16

SHINING THE LIGHT WITHIN

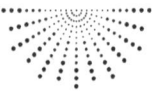

Crystal Timberlake

Many of us grew up in churches where we sang this song over and over and over again. Looking back, I can see myself in my cute little Sunday dress, standing in the children's choir, singing this song, not fully understanding the depth of meaning in those words.

"This little light of mine, I'm gonna let it shine. This little light of mine, I'm going to let it shine… Everywhere I go, I'm gonna let it shine. Let it shine, let it shine, let it shine."

I would find myself humming the tune, and even during the week, the melody would run through my head on repeat.

"This little light of mine I'm gonna let it shine".

I endured many dark days growing up, so letting my light shine was an everyday battle. Homelessness, sexual abuse, rape, domestic violence, an absent father, and a schizophrenic mother made this seemingly small task of *shining* feel unattainable. But this little light of mine, I was going to let it shine NO MATTER WHAT.

Hello, beautiful reader. My name is Crystal J. Timberlake. I'm an International Motivational Speaker, Trauma Informed Transformational Coach, and Published Author. I help women like you, turn pain into purpose through a strategic process that helps you identify how your past was designed to lead you into your purpose. My favorite saying is, "Your devastation is your transportation to your destination". This simple mantra gives power to your inner being and reminds you that no matter what obstacles life throws your way, you were created *with* purpose *on* purpose. Those very moments of crisis were uniquely designed to prepare you for your ultimate goal and purpose.

I am passionate about helping women create their desired lives. While life is happening, we tend to forget about the dreams we used to have as little girls when everything seemed possible. Have you ever found yourself stuck in the monotony of life, doing things because you *should,* but forgetting to take care of yourself and feeling like you've completely abandoned your dreams?

Yes? Well, you are not alone. I've been there before too!

I'm sure you're probably wondering how I went from the girl humming *This Little Light of Mine* to an International Speaker and Transformational Coach for women all across the world. If I am quite honest, sometimes I stop and ask myself that same question. It's been a journey, it's been a process. It's important to remember that journeys begin like a slow-paced marathon, not a sprint. Think about taking a road trip. Part of the driving route requires you to travel through the mountains. While in the mountains you experience high winds, snow, rain, and reduced visibility. You're still excited about your adventure, but for a time you experience fear as well. That doesn't change your desire for all the fun you will experience when you arrive at your destination, but it can shift it out of focus for a while. Deep inside, you know the mountain scare is temporary and sun and fun are just ahead. So again my friend, it's important to enjoy the process of life. Take time to reflect on what you are learning while you adventure.

They say greatness is born in the midst of adversity. I'd add that adversity shows you exactly what you are capable of. In the midst of what other people were thinking should've been the greatest moments of my life - having a baby, celebrating five years of marriage, buying our first house - I realized I simply wasn't happy. I was slipping into a deep depression, and the repetitive nature of everyday life was too much to bear. In that season of great inner turmoil and adversity, I realized that I needed to relinquish and mourn what "was," in order to embrace what "could be". I had to mourn who I had been, who I thought I should be, and the version of me I felt I could never be. On the other side of grief, I had to marry the version of me that was able to see beyond what she could see with her bare eyes. Once I gave birth to this new version of me, then and only then could new possibilities form.

Who was I created to be? Who was I destined to become? What legacy did I want to leave behind? And what will people remember me for?

When I asked myself those questions, I began to come into the fullness of the purpose that I was uniquely created for. In 2016 Boundaries Over Brokenness, LLC was born. Boundaries Over Brokenness is the physical manifestation of giving birth to the possibility of impossibility. After working to develop a new perspective on my life, my passions, and my purpose, an evolution took place within me. To evolve means to transform from something simple to something more complex. I had more drive, more ambition, and I wanted more from life; but more importantly, I understood what my *purpose* was. I had a reason to live. The "new me" felt hopeful about what I could do *for* my life, what I could do *with* my life, and even what I could do in the lives of others.

Even though I created the business in 2016, the road to reprogramming my mindset took time to catch up to the manifestation of owning a business. I had to shed all of the limiting beliefs that wanted to remind me of why this walk wasn't for me. So, I worked with many mindset coaches and business coaches and even went back to therapy. It's a common misconception that we can go from one season to the next without work, support, and development. Let me be the one to remind you, that you can do ANYTHING with the right support, hard work, and dedication.

After doing the internal work, I started to channel my new self-beliefs into building my career and helping women right inside of the corporate walls. I climbed the corporate ladder and committed myself to being the change I wanted to see. Then in 2020, right before the COVID pandemic, I heard a still small voice speak to me, stating it was time to step down from my full-time corporate career and write my first book. It was time to tell the world my story. It was time for me to move into the next phase of my evolution.

Writing my first book, *Boundaries Over Brokenness, A Memoir* was scary, not because it was impossible, but because it was going to expose all my hidden secrets to the world. That was exactly where I needed to start. It was the catalyst for taking the shackles off my voice. Because I told my own story, the good, the bad, and the ugly, I was freed from the fears of what others could possibly say about me. Give yourself permission to unhinge the fear of others telling your story, and tell your own story. Once I did this, I discovered that my most powerful weapon was my voice. I gained the power to speak my truth and to allow my truth to motivate and inspire women who were living through experiences similar to my own. My voice became the light of hope that girls and women like me needed to propel them into purpose. I was finally able to let my light shine and show the world that girls like me deserve EVERYTHING. You, my beautiful reader, deserve everything!

After the success of my book, people began to seek me out to speak on their stages. I am now able to share my story, inspire people, and move others into action, coaching them through pivotal points of transition in their lives. There is only one thing separating you from the life you desire - the one you once dreamed about - and that is your ability to say, "I CHOOSE ME!" One simple decision to choose *you*, the commitment to doing the hard work, and the choice to believe in yourself, will lead you to do things you once thought were impossible. It takes baby steps, my dear reader. One little thing at a time.

One of the most grounding things that I had through the difficult times in my life was my faith. Looking back on the little girl who sang a simple song I realize that it was during that time that I was encouraging myself for a life that had yet to come. After exhausting my own strength when adversity came, I realized at rock bottom that the only thing I could do was surrender. Surrendering to God and stepping out on a mustard seed size faith was key to my process of evolution. Some may believe that having faith will yield an automatic return on investment; it's not quite that simple. Faith is like a muscle, the more you exercise it the more strength you obtain. In your faith walk, you have to start with small seeds of faith, like learning how to follow your own intuition and trusting that everything you need is already within you. Every little bit counts; it all adds up.

The more your faith grows, the more faith God will give you to trust. *To whom much is given, much will be required (Luke 12:48).* This means that you will be held responsible for all that is given. When you step into the shoes of influence you will need every ounce of courage, integrity, and character your process helped you build to walk out your purpose.

So start thinking back to when you were a little girl with all the hope in the world. The dreams seemed endless and you were excited about your future! Sometimes circumstances take away our ability to dream, hope, and see the future. Sometimes life knocks you down and all you can do is get through the day. Sometimes life is simply survival. One incredible thing I've learned about survival is that you don't recognize how bad things were until you get to the other side of it. It's amazing how we adapt mentally, emotionally, and physically no matter what life throws our way. During survival, your hopes and dreams slowly fade away, and all you can do is manage and deal with what's right in front of your face. But it doesn't have to stay that way forever.

Today, I am challenging you to THRIVE! Rise above. Step into your power and start dreaming again. You never know how much strength you have until adversity reveals to you what you are capable of. Stepping out on faith and doing things that you have never seen done is scary. It can be daunting, and on many days you will feel like everything inside of you is a ball of confusion. But every time you challenge yourself to do something different, you allow yourself the opportunity to grow. You reveal new pieces of yourself, and one day you'll look back and see that you're living the life you once only dreamed about.

Always remember, everything you need is *already* within you!

You were created *with* purpose, *on* purpose.

BIO:

Crystal J. Timberlake was raised in Chicago, Il USA and now lives in Minnesota with her husband and son. She began her writing career in 2020 publishing her debut book *Boundaries Over Brokenness, A Memoir*. Since the publication of her memoir, she has also been featured in several collaborative works, spoken on stages all across the world and mentored women through creating their desired lives and identifying their purpose. Crystal is known for her inspirational ability to captivate her audience through sharing her truth and providing practical tips via her speaking and writing. Due to Crystal's traumatic life, she sought out learning the depths of psychology and human behavior, which led her to become a sought-after Speaker, Coach, and Influencer.

www.boundariesoverbrokenness.com

17
HORSE WISDOM FOR WOMEN

Anna Pell

D<span></span>ear Gorgeous Woman,

I wanted to share my own life journey (so far) to show that however lost, unclear, unwell or detached you may feel from your own 'north star' there is always a way to reconnect back to who you are at your essential core.

Your healing journey may be via a meandering path, or one that takes you to places that you never dreamed of visiting. If you have misplaced her, you can return to your authentic, shiny, rich, inner self whenever you are ready or brave enough to venture out to reach for her. Because you always have options; even small tweaks can create kaleidoscopic changes in your life. With new awareness, greater clarity and focus can emerge.

Please be just a tiny bit brave and ask for help and friendship

when you need it - there are women out there who will 'have your back' if only they know you are struggling. And then one day you can help them right back too.
    I am one of those women who 'has your back'.

With love, Anna

Thrive with the Herd
    I work with my beautiful horses helping the amazing women who come to me as clients. My horses and I guide them through their own unique journey so they too can heal and step into their own intuitive, wise-woman skin. This is why I started my horse wisdom for women business, as the horses have so much to teach us about living life on our terms.

I'm here to help women who have struggled like me. Women who want to reconnect to their innate power (gentle or loud) and who want to move to a different chapter in their lives, one that is vibrant, alive and loving. My horses and I help women who:

- Are on auto-pilot in their life or career and want to create a different way of living that helps them move from surviving to real thriving
- Want to connect, or reconnect, more deeply with their inner joy and colourful, vibrant life, celebrating their sensitivity and emotional empathy with others
- Seek emotional healing from a deeply difficult time in their life (eg divorce, ill-health, job loss or depression) and are ready to invest in their deep personal growth and learning

- Want to build a deeper and mutually loving relationship with horses, perhaps having their own horse now or in the past, or simply wanting to connect to these amazing creatures from the ground (non-ridden)

I was all of the above. After three decades of corporate and not-for-profit management consulting work, I was left unwell, exhausted, unmotivated and detached from my inner pilot light. I'd learned to put on a believable façade to those around me but inside I felt hollow. My horses brought me such powerful awareness.

Why Horses

There's something magical about horses and they have always fascinated me; their gentle, compassionate nature and the expressive, glorious beings that they are. With their soft velvety noses and their sassy wiggles when they walk makes me smile deep down inside. I've tried countless times to better understand their essence, that special something that makes them so special to me.

When I was 45 years old my Mum gave me a photo of me aged 5 on the back of a little black and white pony. That was the first I knew of my early childhood horse connection which I've felt has always been with me.

Horses are loving, brave and smart. They have a great sense of humour, live in friendship and community and rarely hold a grudge for more than 3 seconds. Emotion passes through them, they respond, then they go back to grazing. They are such wise teachers for women who have lost their inner pilot light, their north star, or it has been dimmed for too long. When we no longer feel fulfilled in our work, relationships or in our own skin, horses read and reflect back to us everything we need to learn about ourselves in just one soft moment.

They read our body language, muscle tone, emotional state, heart-rate and even our intentions. When we are congruent with our own sense of self and emotional state we come into clearer focus for the horse; we become more trustworthy to them when we outwardly and respectfully express our true inner state.

When we become quiet inside and listen to our needs the horse's wisdom speaks out. We experience a shift in our emotional and physical state that allows our inner desires to emerge and our limiting blocks to be revealed. From this deeply experiential process we can catapult ourselves towards a well-deserved and joyful future.

Me, a career woman?

I didn't especially plan to be a career woman. In my 20s I loved the buzz and excitement of working in the West End of London. I travelled lots, worked hard, partied hard, life was exciting and an adventure.

I excelled as a management consultant, working in corporate, not-for-profit and central/local government sectors. I loved what I did, helping managers and their teams work exceptionally well together, using my deep intuition and powerful insights to help bring out their talents and knowledge in their chosen fields through leadership coaching and organisational change.

In my 30s I completed my Masters in Business Administration (MBA) whilst working full-time as a change management consultant. I was paid well but there was very little 'me time'. At weekends I'd get home exhausted, sleep, do chores and then the merry-go-round would start up again every Monday. Quality romantic relationships were limited; I didn't have the time or energy and any that were longer-term were rarely supportive or good for me.

Over the next few years, I slowly and gradually lost my joy and motivation for doing what I once loved. The working culture and environments generally did not support me, or the people I was helping, in our own growth and learning. I saw talented men and women struggling to cope in jobs they felt obligated to stay in for financial or other reasons – not because they deeply enjoyed their work.

A change of pace

I had started to explore how to shift my career to one that had more meaning and purpose, with a special focus on how I could help women in the workplace. This exploration included rekindling my passion for horses and fascination with how they thought and behaved. I trained in 'natural horsemanship' and 'horse whispering'. This is about how we impact the horse and how, by dramatically slowing down, we can better hear their needs and consequently our own.

A chance accident when a horse jumped on my foot (it really did hurt) meant I was in a plaster-cast for 6 weeks whilst most of the physical healing took place. A close friend lent me a book called *"The Tao of Equus – a Woman's Journey of Healing and Transformation through the Way of the Horse"* by Linda Kohanov. Her story spoke to me so deeply and at a soul-level that I immediately knew I wanted to train as an equine facilitated coach.

A year later I joined Linda's unique and highly skilled training for women alongside horses in Tucson, Arizona that created a powerful connection for me with a community of women in the United States. We each explored our way out of darkness and loss - towards rejuvenation, hope and deep personal and professional change.

Then, at age 39, halfway through my training, I was diagnosed with breast cancer. The year-long training with the horses and my fellow group of women held me throughout my crisis, alongside my family and close friends in the UK. It was one of the hardest times of my life, one that I could soon look back on as the darkest but most rewarding time for growth.

Waking up from auto-pilot

Before my cancer diagnosis, my personal development had been akin to a gentle flowing stream. From day 1 of my diagnosis my growth and learning shifted dramatically to the speed of Niagara Falls; fast, chaotic, life threatening and a force of nature. It forced me to step back from my full-on working life. I started to re-evaluate who I was, what mattered to me, and what gave me real joy and deep satisfaction - personally and professionally. I dealt with deep depression, soul-loss and struggled to cope on very many levels.

It was the horses who kept me alive and sane, along with the 2 rescue dogs I adopted – or rather, who adopted me.

I spent the next 10 years in my 40s on auto-pilot as I was financially obliged to go back into the corporate workplace, albeit on a freelance basis. I took long periods of downtime between each contract when I recovered from the corporate madness and, once rested, I would coach women and groups alongside horses doing what I knew was my 'calling' in life. One by one my 3 beautiful horses came into my care – Millie, Del Boy and Bertie, and more recently Tallulah, a friend's pony.

And then Covid arrived, and my consulting contracts stopped completely. I was diagnosed with a chronically under active thyroid which explained my ongoing exhaustion for sure. Then followed a realisation that my menopause symptoms in my 50s were now so extreme I failed to thrive on any level. Brain fog, severe muscle aches, more exhaustion, major hot flushes – the list went on. After 6 years of hellish menopause symptoms after being told by a former GP that Hormone Replacement Therapy (HRT) was not an option for me because of my history with breast cancer, I found a private GP and menopause advocate who specialised in plant-based, bio-identical HRT. Within 3 months I felt better and within 6 months I felt I'd become a new improved version of myself.

A new venture with horses

My emerging health, energy and self-belief gave me the conviction to end the years of procrastination in creating the unique job of my dreams. I invested in a creative, online coach who works with women entrepreneurs – and yes, I'm beginning to feel like I just might be one!

Working towards any authentic, personal (and indeed professional) change is a slow-shifting process, as one of my close women friends has just shared with me. I'm still in that process and wow, I so enjoy the slower, 'horse-time' grazing pace.

My heart-felt thank you to all the horses. I've spent all these years trying to find out more about the essence of horses – and along the way I've been shown how to heal myself and share this healing wider with my 'tribe' of women. If you are in need of it I hope my story offers insight and hope; and most definitely reveals some small truth about the wonderful nature of horses.

BIO:

Anna's own journey of healing with horses has helped her make sense of the dark and difficult times in her life, moving towards a more rooted, happier life. Her 30 years in corporate and not-for-profit work as a change management consultant enabled her to specialise in mentoring women and in guiding others to lead their own change.

Her love and passion for horses has been a constant theme in her life, always wanting to learn more about their essential nature. Hanging out with her horses and dogs is Anna's happy place. Encouraging other women to find their happy place with *'Thrive with the Herd – Horse Wisdom for Women'* is the real gift that her horses offer us.

Anna offers 1:1 and group coaching for women alongside her horses, from which deep self-awareness and personal freedom can emerge. Her four horses and two rescue terriers are ready and waiting to help you thrive further in life.

www.thrivewiththeherd.co.uk

18

3 THINGS I'VE LEARNT IN MY FIRST YEAR AS A MOMPRENEUR

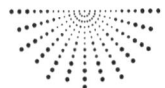

Jan Daudi

As a woman who gave up two teaching jobs at the height of her career to become a full time homemaker, I can say that the shift in mindset to take the leap into the unknown world of business life was a big challenge for me. Being the queen of my castle in control of a predictable day was very comforting. I had my dream existence of a big happy family life, with caring and intelligent people around me everyday respecting and honouring all of my efforts.

Academics have always been a big part of my life growing up and so expanding my knowledge was never questioned as important. Therefore starting my masters degree in journalism when my youngest child was 6 years old was easily arranged. However, my circumstances as a married woman who did not have an essential need to work meant that turning my talents towards the pursuit of business opportunities required a more conscious reasoning process. Why should I add to my life work program when there was no obvious need? Would my home life be compromised? Am I not too old to start a business adventure when many would be thinking of retiring? The timing of my entrepreneurial adventure was also quite significant in that COVID had arrived and turned all the known laws of reality upside down. The odds seemed squarely stacked against me as a woman and mother. It was cited in an article by Forbes contributor Georgene Huang (January 2022) that half of all women in the workplace were losing confidence at work. Of those, 75% expressed that the reasons for this were financial setbacks and loss of career traction over the last two years of the Pandemic.

Here are the 3 key learnings that I have realised over the last 12 months as a mompreneur during the last year of COVID in full force. I'm writing this chapter at a time when women are emerging out of a political health storm that has impacted their lives at a level that is unprecedented in recent history.

Managing the motherhood mindset

Dedicating 22 years to raising my 5 children (without childcare facilities, partly home schooling and living as an expat wife with few friends) hardwired me to put other people's needs first. Finding myself in a space where my growing kids had more independence, I was encouraged to pursue my own skill sets and ambitions outside of my home life.

My Masters degree in journalism led me to new communications platforms where women asked me to coach them. My capacity to be paid for my talents emerged organically and quite by chance. Entering into groups and mentoring dynamics where my technical skills were nurtured placed me in a new "family ecosystem" and I found myself automatically showing up as "Mum" to everyone. Having parented my younger siblings resulted in a higher propensity for self abandonment. My own goals were side-lined and there was no one around me aware or willing enough to intervene. I was so busy nurturing everyone else I increasingly found myself living vicariously through others celebrating their wins after my hundreds of hours in free coaching "gifts". I knew that this was an unsustainable business model, but admitting my circumstances would make me look mentally incompetent. Worse still, my engagements started to look odd as people thought "What is she getting out of this?".

Other mothers online expressed the struggles of balancing maternal personality types and personal development. Mummy guilt is real, and the feeling that you may be letting your family down by looking after interests outside the home is a constant battle for many mothers returning to work ambitions. There is very little written about the psychology of this workplace phenomenon, any managers looking to help mothers in teams may find Jordan Peterson lecture entitled "The Mind of Highly (Dis-)Agreeable People, helpful. He theorised that a women's nervous systems are designed for the immense sacrifices required in selflessly looking after infants who must have their needs catered to unquestionably in their early years. He describes how the perfect person to "exploit" in a career or business context was a highly functioning middle aged "agreeable mother personality" type (compassionate, selfless, polite, hardworking). Place such a person in the service of adult men who tend to be "dis-agreeable" in the personality spectrum (blunt in their communication styles, competitive, tough minded) then you have a circumstance that will most certainly place women at a disadvantage.

Whilst it was good to know I was not insane, I personally looked deeper within my belief systems and found clear direction that being a Muslim woman and mother who has a business, had no contradiction. Balance should be sought and amassing immense success with your family needs met and not sacrificed in the process, is an act of worship. It was this revelation that now serves me in becoming the optimal mother, wife and businesswoman I can be.

Self-made safe spaces

The other key area of my business journey learning process was understanding that curating safe spaces is my responsibility. The term "Safe Space" is popular with millennials and I have found it to be one of the most mis-used and abused in popular culture. The problem here is that a "safe space" has no unified meaning socially and it is completely subjective to an individual's understanding of what are acceptable behaviours and what the people in a group will tolerate without holding others accountable.

Double standards where an authority figure has one standard and a client / employee has another (being lower ranking in the perceived power dynamics) creates a toxic business culture. What I have come to understand from exploring beyond the highly controlled, loving and respectful "safe space" of my own home is, do not expect anyone to understand how you want to be treated. Morals will always be subjective and second to monetary gain for most people, so you have to be responsible for your own moral compass. A key learning for me is never assume anyone will act in defence of your person. Bystander apathy is more common than outspoken bravery. I've experienced women stay silent in the face of my violations and place loyalty with money interests. Authority figures will expect you to tolerate "authentic free expression" but few will tolerate you standing up to defend yourself or calling out abusive behaviour. Be prepared to be labelled "difficult" or "un-coachable", it comes with the territory of being an independent thinker who is not easily controlled. Celebrate these labels as affirmation that you are an empowered soul!

There is no right or wrong in what makes you able to thrive

and not just survive. This is for you to define and others to accept. If they do not value you enough to honour your beliefs in practice, then it's evidence that you are not in a safe space and you are not welcome. Read every word of your contracts and discuss anything that does not align with what you want openly and clearly. When you find yourself compromised, use the official private channel of complaints and document all communications as you don't know the crisis management protocols and if there is best practice. Before investing in the best mentors, or working out your 3 year growth projections, know your values. The personality profits that will result will serve in incalculable ways making you less easy to manipulate or play small. Of course, your values are personal to you and it's not for me to tell you the framework here, but as an example of parameters, you should know where you stand in, for example, how your personal data should be used, how you wish to be represented in your identity or what verbal, non-verbal or physical communications styles make you comfortable or not.

With my values clear, I knew that I had no reason to settle for less than I deserve and that my true tribe of supporters would celebrate me, not just tolerate me. Standing alone in dignity will alway be better than crawling in a crowd. Fear and scarcity mindsets where you can't even trust yourself and your own judgement will never ever lead you to the correct purpose in life, which is the true meaning of greatness in the human condition.

Your network is your safety net

The final lesson I can share in my first 12 months as a mompreneur relates to your network and the people you surround yourself with. I would like to shift the perspective that your "Network is your net worth". My personal experience this past year resonates more with the fact that you are sufficient in your net worth as a creation of the Almighty. Anything additional to your identity and its enhancement is welcome in the already established completeness of your being.

What I have experienced is that my network and networking skills have allowed me to grow, learn and accelerate my business life in amazing ways, only when I am mindful of my intentions and exercise a super selective process where my values and purpose in life is un-compromised. There is a danger in the early years of your business life to feel the need to say "yes" to every "expert" promising to deliver your dreams. There is also a tactical narrative where many may state they are the "only way", or "the best" and without their help there is certain failure. The fact is there are many routes to success within any niche in life. The focus should be clarity on what you want, your "why", your non-negotiable standard operating procedures in life. Where is the REAL evidence that a personality can actually deliver on what they say? Integrity and proof through validated testimonies can help you know if you should bring someone into your network. Be aware that partial testimonies from people that have not fully engaged in a service cannot be taken as proof of someone's service. Powerful testimonies exist from people that may have had problems with a service, who then find satisfaction with how their complaint was solved with good manners and great customer service care.

Your family should never be left at the sidelines of your network! Include them in the process and enjoy it with them. After all, you spend most of your time in the process! The ups and the downs can be great bonding tools. I have found that when the betrayals and false friends appear, your core team will always be there for you. Expect your network to flux and change. My greatest advocates to date have been the ones I invested the least money in. Their sincere concern for me spoke volumes in their personal DM's and unpaid zoom calls that navigated me through some of my greatest hardships. There are

CEOs of Forbes ranked companies that I know are the real deal and those that are great at marketing with little humanitarian substance.

All of these examples have definitely served me to know the kind of business woman I want to be and ultimately the best kind of legacy I want to leave when my children teach their children about their grandmother's life. I look forward to reaping that priceless investment opportunity more than any other corporate accolade.

BIO:

Jan Daudi is a Cambridge University certified communications coach using her psychology and journalism degrees to help women;

"Say what they mean, mean what they say, without being mean"

Media mentoring is also available in her bespoke programs as she has had her own live talk show and is certified in the performing arts.

As an international public speaker she was featured as one of the top 100 women making entrepreneurial impact in Africa. She is the founder and CEO of MissCommuniTeam and her coaching programs are available for purchase online and in 1:1 elite contracts.

www.facebook.com/coachjandaudi

19
IS YOUR LIFE ALIGNED WITH YOUR VALUES?

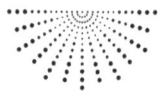

Kate Humphreys

Are you living true to your values? I wasn't and it led me to burnout, frustration, resentment and a pretty miserable time. It's so easy to find yourself on a path and just trudge the same groove each day as it becomes so ingrained, so habitual, that we can forget that we have a choice.

Growing up, I was a determined, outspoken individual with a strong character and an indomitable spirit. My parents were hard working, entrepreneurial and determined to carve out their slice of the good life (I wonder where I get it from?). They owned several businesses and always put in a full day and often a full evening of work to keep us fed and clothed. I learned by example, about a work ethic which included hard work and plenty of grit and determination. I developed a personal creed to do it the best that I can, perfection meant I just had to reach a little further than I thought that I could.

Later, I trained to become a teacher and of course, I was determined to be the best I could. And I was. I did really, really well and loved what I was doing. I'm a lifelong learner and I would spend any spare time reading educational pedagogy books and swotting up on new ideas and strategies I could use with my classes.

Over the next few years I would go through a series of miscarriages and ectopic pregnancies and came to the sad conclusion that my husband and I would not enjoy the experience of being parents. As a consolation prize we opted for a large house we could barely afford and thought if we can't have a baby, we can at least indulge in a nice home.

Within three months, I was once again pregnant. We worried through the entire pregnancy that we would lose our baby but fortune turned its face favourably upon us and our perfect little boy arrived in our lives. I finally felt that I was whole, and that all my wishes had been granted. When I gazed upon the bluest eyes I had ever seen, I promised to love him forever and spend all my time being the best mum I could be.

Jump ahead a few years. I'm so happy being a mum but I'm burnt out and miserable with my work. After nearly 20 years of teaching and burning the candle at both ends for far too long, I felt like I was getting nowhere. I was tired and frustrated by having a job which required me to put other people's children first. There was a viral quote which perfectly summed it up for me:

'Why are women expected to work like they don't have children and mother like they don't work?'

Sometimes we need something to move us, to change us, to wake us up, to get us to listen to our heart again. The catalyst for the beginning of my paradigm shift, unfortunately, was the death of my mother. She had been my biggest supporter, my source of wisdom and my go-to advisor when I needed help with a decision. She always seemed to know the right answer and when she was gone, I felt adrift and lost. She was my compass and suddenly my compass was gone.

After a lot of soul searching and grieving, I decided to take positive action. I was lucky enough to work in a school which funded a wellbeing coach. A few days later I found myself sitting in front of a counsellor. A wellness coach by the name of Amanda. She is a wonderful woman who changed my life and gave me the tools to work around my grief and accept the loss. She introduced me to Positive Psychology and gave me a different way of looking at the world.

People think that it takes months and years to bring around huge shifts, but mine happened in an instant. As soon as I took back my power, I understood that I am totally and completely in charge of my life and so are you.

Amanda woke me up and allowed me to see the rutted path that I was sleepwalking through each day, she allowed me to verbalise my values and design the life of my dreams. She allowed me to see that I could be whoever I wanted to be and that teaching until I retired at 67 was not the only choice I had.

And so I dreamt, and journalled, created vision boards and told the universe that things needed to change. That I wanted to be a Mum before anything else and have the freedom to work when I wanted. On my first vision board I created I added:

- Work from home
- More quality time with my family
- Have a dog
- Brand new car
- Holiday to Bali
- Replace teaching salary

I still have the vision board pinned to my noticeboard. I look at it everyday and remember making it, thinking that these were pipedreams and not based in my reality.

But, as I consistently put into practice the strategies I was learning, the things I had 'manifested' in my mind were actually manifesting in my life. Things like being able to work from home, replacing my teacher's salary and very quickly, surpassing even that. I had envisioned being able to get a dog and most importantly, I had manifested being able to spend more time with my son. All of these goals have been achieved. They were manifested. Apart from a trip to Bali, thanks Covid!

I needed to get out of my rut and for me that meant changing what I do. I sat at my computer and googled 'Ways to make money from home'. We've all done that right? My eyes were opened to the world of online business and I created a second income through Virtual Assistant work. It used my existing skill sets and very soon I found it necessary to expand my skills, to learn new ones and I discovered that I enjoyed this very much. I was really very good at it ... but it wasn't enough.

There was something more out there for me but I just had to figure out what it was. I had to learn to listen to my heart again. I came across a book about Online Business Managers and it was like it spoke to my soul!

My next move was to become a certified Online Business Manager and I learned all about systems, operations, digital marketing, launch planning, funnels, automations and how to scale a business. I worked with some inspirational coaches at the top of their field and learnt so much from each one.

A serendipitous meeting led to me enrolling in a Positive Psychology Coaching programme and with this it felt like another piece of the jigsaw slotted into place. Positive Psychology changed my entire life in a moment and I wanted to be able to support other women to experience this shift.

When I set out to achieve my "best life", I wasn't aiming for wealth or fame. For me, it was simply a deep rooted need to spend more quality time with my family. (Okay, maybe a little bit of wealth. After all, my best life included more holiday time.)

My son and husband have always supported me and encouraged me. In fact it was my son who pressed send on my resignation email as I was hesitating and allowing fear to control me!

As I write this I am still on the upwards swing of manifestation. I have envisioned working with amazing people and the universe has responded. My clients are some of the best people I could hope to work with and my influence on their businesses and being able to support them as they scale, brings me so much joy. I can see how a positive mindset, a belief in one's self and having an open arms approach to accepting the opportunities offered and encountered in day to day life increases the value of not only a business but the value of self.

My roles vary with each of my clients, as each of them requires different strategies to enable them to live their best life. Some I help with making their systems more efficient, others I help to increase the recurring revenue in their business with new offers and programmes. More recently, I have been using my educational background to redesign online courses and bring gamification to engage their learners.

I offer positivity, support and encouragement to each of my clients. I help each of these wonderful and talented women uncover what their own natural talents are if they cannot see them. I help them to realise their own entrepreneurial visions and how it can be possible to have an incredibly successful and profitable business without it running you into the ground.

Using my Holistic Systems® methodology I help them to focus on the parts of the business which bring them joy and stop them feeling like an employee in their own business. And I want that for you as well.

If you have a dream in your heart then it can be a reality. As Bob Proctor said 'If you can see it in your mind, you can hold it in your hand'. If you are sleepwalking through your life, then it's time to wake up and take control. And it's never too late to start!

- Be brave and say yes to the things that scare you!
- Use affirmations and be aware of your inner talk
- Surround yourself with people who encourage you to grow
- Spend time dreaming of your best life
- Find out what brings you joy and do more of that
- Understand your values and how you can live them each day

BIO:

Kate Humphreys is a former science teacher turned certified Online Business Manager & Positive Psychology Coach. She recently featured in The American Reporter as one of 'The Top 10 Online Business Managers to Watch in 2022'.

Kate supports small business owners to thrive, find joy and freedom in their business by implementing systems and strategies to streamline business operations.

Working together using her Holistic Systems® methodology, you will have access to a blend of business strategy, positive psychology interventions, mindset and systems support. Kate supports you to envisage your best life, find your zone of genius and design your business to achieve your life goals.

www.katehumpherys.com

20
FROM SALES TO SEX THERAPIST

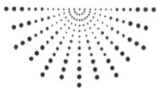

Nicola Foster

Last year I turned 50.
What a fantastic opportunity to reflect on my working life to date!

When I finished university back in 1993, I landed a 'milk round' graduate job in retail. I had the company car, I had management responsibility, and I quickly learned how to navigate office politics and competition with my peers. After a few years I moved on to an advertising agency, and then into various sales and strategic marketing roles in US-owned publishing companies. The hours were long and it was a 'work hard, play hard' culture.

But something just wasn't right for me. I didn't know it then, but what I can see looking back is that my core qualities as a human were not valued in the organisational culture of these big companies. Empathy, kindness, softness, gentleness; these were all seen as signs of weakness, and I learned to be colder, less emotional, more professional.

I was also plagued by the sense that what I was doing wasn't making any difference in the world. I was making the company some money, continually chasing quarterly results and nothing more.

It felt meaningless.

I recall one particularly bad time being bullied by a manager who used a lot of emotional manipulation to psychologically undermine everyone in their team. When I tried to address this with Human Resources I learned an interesting lesson about power in organisations. I made the decision to become self-employed one day, to be able to write my own destiny and become my own boss.

At that time I was a single woman with a mortgage to pay. Retraining for a new career felt like quite a mountain to climb. And I really didn't know what it was I wanted to do.

So I began the slow and steady process of trying to decide what my next chapter would be. I read a lot of career books - remember *'What Colour Is Your Parachute?'* anyone?

Because I felt that there wasn't a lot of good help available for people who wanted to do something different with their lives, I decided to retrain as a career coach. I did a part time postgraduate degree at Birkbeck, University of London whilst still working. This was a brave and wise decision - I loved the academic rigour of the study, meeting amazing new people, and beginning to see myself a-fresh as someone with skills and knowledge.

It was around this time that I also discovered personal development workshops around themes of relationship and sexual intimacy. I worked with an amazing and inspiring teacher, Jan Day. Through my work with Jan my life opened up in exciting new ways. I met a whole new friendship circle of interesting people who shared my own commitment to a path of growth, presence, embodiment and living life with full attention.

I also started talking-therapy and, feeling its benefits, became drawn to the idea of becoming a therapist myself. I found a path to healing the layers of relationship trauma that were held in my body after my partner suddenly went missing when I was 30. Carl Jung talks about the notion of the 'wounded healer', and it was my own traumatic relationship loss that catapulted me into this period of personal exploration, expansion, and growth.

So, in 2013/2014 I began retraining as a relationship and sex therapist. Once again I was studying whilst working full time. Most of my disposable income was spent on books, training, and travelling up and down to London for study. Foreign holidays and fancy meals out became a thing of the past. I went on to complete a two-year placement supporting NHS referral clients with psychosexual issues at the Local Counselling Centre in Hertfordshire. I will be forever grateful for the faith they showed in me and the opportunity to learn within a supportive team - thank you so much, Julie!

My full-time employment now is supporting couples struggling with all sorts of issues – from dealing with mismatched desire, to recovering from an affair, or navigating open relationships. I also help individuals who want to make sense of break-ups and who want to create new, healthy relationships. I absolutely love seeing the transformations people make. My clients often arrive at therapy feeling broken and in distress. Watching them leave feeling more hopeful and more optimistic is very rewarding.

An aside - one of my few regrets in life is that I didn't get therapy when I was so broken at the age of 30 because I thought I couldn't afford it. I could, had I spent less on Marks and Spencers' ready meals and rounds in the pub, and it would have transformed my life so much sooner. If you think you would benefit, move heaven and earth to make it happen – a good therapist can truly transform your life.

My new work is such a privilege and joy. People entrust me with their innermost lives. I treat that with honour and respect. I learn so much from my client's wide and varied life experiences and learnings. I am also constantly researching and reading in my field, devouring books on a weekly basis, loving to learn from my respected peers and amazing well-known experts such as Esther Perel, Stan Tatkin and Ellyn Bader.

I am passionate about offering online classes and courses as a way of being able to serve people who can't come to therapy in person. I love the creative challenge of making complex information simple and clear. I'm inspired by taking people on a journey from feeling lost around their relationships to feeling happier and more empowered. I incorporate brilliant ways of working such as the Voice Dialogue method from Hal and Sidra Stone, which is such an enlivening and rich way of exploring the unconscious patterns we all have. I also love working with the Initiator/Inquirer process I learnt with Ellyn Bader, helping couples build trust so they can support each other's growth as individuals as well as strengthening their relationship.

I feel very fortunate to come from a long career in marketing. It hasn't been too daunting for me to know how to do things like creating a website, writing copy and briefing designers. In my first working week I placed some Google ads, hired a room close to the British Museum and soon I was a busy working therapist. I almost always have a waiting list because I get a lot of repeat clients and word of mouth recommendations.

What has been much more of a journey for me is learning how to get to grips with things like Instagram at the age of 50. I am super grateful to business mentors, like the lovely Gemma Went, who teach me so much about making an online business work. As well as learning about the technical, strategic and tactical aspects of growing an online offering, Gemma's teaching also works with my mindset through energy work to help shift unconscious blocks. Each week I do breathwork, EFT and guided visualisations to help me work through things like 'imposter syndrome' and upper limiting beliefs.

Having spent most of my life as a salaried employee it has also been a challenge to learn how to do bookkeeping and self-assessment tax returns.

Overall, my biggest business challenge is time management. There are so many aspects of the work to factor in - as well as being the CEO, you're the PA, the marketing manager, the communications manager, the accountant, the finance director, the sales rep and the tea lady. It would be easy to work 24 hours a day. A constant learning is how to set boundaries between work and play and have enough time to kick back, rest and have fun.

The other challenge is isolation. I am fortunate that my partner is also interested in the field of sexuality and relationships and we have had a lot of fun recording our podcast, Intimacy Matters, but I do miss laughing over cups of tea in the communal kitchens of office life.

The absolute best part of being self-employed? The freedom to create my own working schedule. I recently reduced my clinic days from 4 to 3. Now I work with clients Monday to Wednesday, and I use Thursday to work the administration side of the business. I give myself Friday as a day for me – that might be an 'artist date' (if you know the Artist's Way by Julia Cameron), or a day going down for a wild swim at the coast in Dorset or exploring the local area all around me in the beautiful Somerset Levels. I love seeking out new farm shops and bakeries and indulging my foodie side!

I started my business in January 2018. I'm coming up on five years as a self-employed therapist. So, what does the future hold?

Something that I'm really looking forward to is enjoying

more of the creative aspects of working for myself. I'm finally getting the hang of making reels on Instagram and it can be quite exciting to see something you create being enjoyed. I'm also planning to write a book about intimacy as a challenge to find my voice.

My main intention for the next five years is to continue to develop and grow my signature program for people who want to overcome blocks to intimacy. It's for couples who don't want to drift apart and who want to discover and practise new ways of communicating and playing together. Partners who want to feel intimate and at ease with each other, who want to support each other's growth and happiness as individuals. I teach about how we can help to calm each other's nervous systems and reduce stress so we can thrive. I offer inspiration for how to have better, more high quality, more magnificent sex and pleasure in midlife.

I'm also loving holding in person 2-day intensives. Meeting a couple and spending two full days together is so transformational. We can really explore intimacy with communication, relaxation, and movement, enjoying depth and having fun at the same time. I work a lot with a model called the Wheel of Consent by Dr Betty Martin and these two-day sessions give us time to really explore the dynamics of the wheel properly. I'm also looking forward to continuing to run in person intimacy and relationship workshops with my partner Jason. We run group events in London and Somerset and it's a fantastic opportunity to explore relationship and intimacy in a group space, and to dance, move, meditate and BE together in a loving community. This is the essence of my work and my life; Love, Community, and Connection.

If you are at a crossroads wondering whether to leap into a life where you are in the driving seat... I say 'do it'! It's full of challenges but waking up on a Monday excited to go to 'work' makes it all worthwhile.

BIO:

Hi, I'm Nicola Foster, Relationship and Intimacy Coach. I offer therapy, coaching and workshops where you can learn, explore, and develop new skills on how to enjoy more empowered and conscious intimate relationships. My favourite aspect of my work is supporting new and long-term couples to discover how they can build or deepen intimacy and trust with each other. I'm passionate about this because when we can connect with each other safely, we are happier, more relaxed, and more able to cope with life's challenges and ups and downs.

I'm based in the south-west of the UK near Glastonbury where I live with my partner Jason and indulge my passions for immersion in water walking in the woods deepening my meditation and yoga practices and conscious movement and dance. And if all that sounds a little bit worthy some of my other passions include Michelin star food and fancy pants cocktails served in really cold glasses!

www.realrelating.com/workwithme

21
THE FINAL BOW

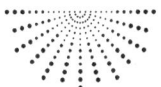

Lana O'Brien

I look back now and I remember the last time I took a bow, the lights, the 1000's of people in the audience cheering loudly, the adrenaline coursing through my body! There's no feeling like this on the planet... well to me anyway. The thing Is you never know it's your final bow at the time.

Having danced since the age of 3, I was so fortunate to have a career in the Musical Theatre and dance world when I got older. Training hard in dance college, to then being thrust into the London audition scene in the 90's wasn't one for the faint hearted. Countless auditions of being told you're too fat, too small, not pretty enough or just not good enough. Then you brush yourself up and go work in some random job, all so you can eat, pay your rent and get to the next audition.

Jobs would vary from being a hostess at corporate events, handing out free treats from some food brand or not so glam of handing out flyers where people don't dare look you in the eye... or even better you're handing them out dressed as anything from a Jockey to a life size orange, I've done it all!

This life was mine and 1000's of others all waiting and wanting to be part of the magical dance world! It takes grit, determination and pure passion... with a little bit of the childhood magic and vision fuelling you to keep going. I look back and realise I was blessed to work as a dancer AND as a singer in dance videos, different dance shows all over the world and a famous west end musical by QUEEN for many years! But what they never prepare you for is the last time.

You see it's definitely an industry with an age timeline, like any athlete I suppose. And at the ripe old age of 29 as I stood at the back of a class at Pineapple studio's, I just took a moment. It was a usual fast paced class of spins and kicks and although I could still do it all, (just about!) I knew my hips and my body would ache much longer afterwards. I looked at the younger dancers and felt something in me that made me realise it was time to hang up the shoes! It was their world now and it was time to bow out. I was ready for some normality in my life, whatever that meant!

So now what?! The thing about the dance world is it prepares you more than you know for the 'real world'. Yes pirouettes and shuffle ball change on a CV don't help for an office job, BUT the continuous self-promotion, bounce back ability and non-stop determination, I now realise, are the lifelong skills we all need!

I did what I knew best and did everything at once. I left the bright lights of London and moved back to the beautiful south coast of England, my home town. I started up a wedding dance company, this was now 2010 and the infamous "first dance fever" was in full swing. I worked in schools teaching dance, I signed up to become a Zumba teacher.... Something I am still rocking out to 5 times a week! I worked in a bar pulling pints AND one of the biggest life shifts to happen that summer was.... I joined a Network Marketing company. I truly believe when you are open to opportunity and trusting that the universe / the higher power or whatever you like to call it is guiding you, things will open up in front of you. Paths will show you a way that you didn't even see were there before.

That summer of 2010 I sat with my friend, another performer and she told me all about this wellness brand. You see I had suffered right through my 20's with adult acne. It was something I had battled with for a long time and I was prescribed the medication Roaccutane 3 times in my 20s! If you know about this drug and the side effects, 1 time is bad enough but 3 was just crazy! Anyway, my friend gave me some products to try and as mad as this sounds, in a week my skin had completely cleared!* So naturally this caught my attention, what was in and what was not in these products? I jumped into the business right away, if not only for the bigger discount I thought what the hell, I'll just add it into all the other things I am doing!

I quickly learnt that everyone had an opinion on the Network Marketing industry, but do you know what, that is ok!

The resilience from the rejections in the dancing days before was going to help me massively. Not everyone wants to be in the 9-5 and that is ok, not everyone has the stamina for their own business and that too is ok!

What I have seen in 12 years growing an online business on a huge scale, is the massive growth in the digital age that you have to be a part of if you want to evolve! That working time-smart not harder is the best way, meaning looking at multiple income streams. That having leveraged income and having a business where people can shop your brand without you needing to do anything on that transaction is HUGE! That using your social media space for people to see who you are, like a living breathing CV is also huge! So so much has changed in 12 years and the online space is massive for any woman wanting to scale their business.

But yes I hear you cry, I get it the online/ digital world is important...Isn't it better to be in person?

Of course it is when you can , but if you're not using any social media space it is only going to get bigger so you need to start now.

The next thing more important than anything, is to evolve and grow your mindset if you want to be successful!

My journey with personal development began in 2010 when I picked up the book The Success Principles by Jack Canfield. I highly recommend this by the way! I travelled to seminars in Vegas to see Tony Robbins, John Maxwell, Mel Robbins, Rachel Hollis, Richard Branson and sooooo many more, my hunger for learning about how you are actually in control of it all, grew.

How you react, what you do, how you respond to events around you. How you show up, how you bounce back, how you move forward, how you grow, how you trust the universe, how you lean into your own super power, which is of course, YOU! Reading any good personal development is such a great investment into yourself I can't recommend it enough!

From books it moved to audios, YouTube videos and of course now Podcasts. The wellness movement was growing faster than ever through 2010 to 2022 as was the thirst for mental wellness and growth too. Another pivotal point in my journey was the teachings in the book The Miracle Morning by Hal Elrod. This is another high recommendation that you need to read immediately if you haven't! How you start your day can dictate your ENTIRE day! When you learn about simple breathing techniques, meditation, affirmations and the power of gratitude.... I can 100% say you will never be the same person again. I am so pleased that in my business we focus on this together hosting a BE WELL call every morning! It's truly game changing.

So, I'm saying the online space is important. The want to grow your mindset is as important. But a big thing I see that lacks in women more than anything... is the last piece of the puzzle! What is it?? It's the belief in yourself that you can do anything! If you can believe you can do it then you're 99% of the way there. Having worked closely with 100's of women over the past 12 years in fitness and business I know this is the secret ingredient to it all.

These last 12 years took me through the journey of becoming a step-mum and a mummy too. Building my Zumba and dance fitness business to be the biggest it can be. To then see me growing a network marketing business to the top 2% in our company globally! My efforts on all of these things make me the proudest still today, alongside the most important role of Mumma.

Through the years I faced heartbreak, grief of losing my father, faced injury, being unable to work and many more twists and turns in this wickedly wonderful life we live. The 2 years after 2020 and to current day took us all through the most catastrophic global events we ever knew possible. The toughest there have been with loss on every scale but what became clear was the need for community was stronger than ever.

We never know when it's the Final Bow in any career. But what I know for sure is that it will always work out exactly as it's meant too. I believe life is what you make it, I believe life is too short to not forgive. I believe we all have a magic that runs deep inside us...all we have to do is believe in that magic and lean into it!

Stay Fabulous

Lana x

*Skincare story is a personal testament and not a medical claim.

BIO:

Lana is an Independent consultant and Vice president with the wellness brand Arbonne. She is also a high energy Zumba and dance teacher and has been since 2010. She lives on the south coast of the UK in Hampshire with her family and loves living by the sea in the town she grew up in.

She loves nothing more than helping women to see how amazing they are either in dance, fitness or business. It's her passion to help 1000s more see that the magic is inside them already.

www.lanaobrien.arbonne.com

22
HAVING IT ALL

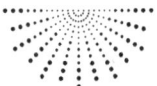

Sarah Fisher

As a mum, I wanted it all. A successful career, a comfortable lifestyle, financial security and to be around for my son. To be able to attend sports days, go on school trips, do the school run and just be around as he grew up. Something I had from my mum.

Working full time for someone else just wasn't going to enable that to happen. Yes, I'd have the comfortable lifestyle, financial security and probably still have a successful career but I'd be stressed trying to balance that with being a mum.

And as an adoptive mum it was even harder, and my son needed more support. He was 7 when we became a family and my life changed forever, for the better.

After my adoption leave, I went back to work part time. It was a busy, stressful senior role. I loved it (most of the time!), but something had changed inside me. My intention had been to build back up to full time, but I quickly realised that wasn't going to work. After 9 months of trying, I decided to leave and, whilst I retrained, started a consultancy company.

For me, retraining was the best thing I could have done. I closed the consultancy company and I'm now a full-time parent coach working with families who are struggling to connect. I work with a huge range of families and struggles but specialise in child to parent violence and helping families whose children are neurodivergent. I've been doing it for 7 years and love it. It's not easy, but it's so rewarding.

Where am I now?

I have 3 employed staff who help me run the business. They are fantastic. I put off employing people for ages, but it's been the best thing for both the business *and* my sanity! I also have a team of associate coaches, who all bring their own brilliance and breadth of knowledge. With them, we are able to help more families across the UK and internationally and that's my goal as we continue to grow. I've also been able to reduce my hours slightly which is great. It's meant I have more time with my son and more time to enjoy life.

How did I get here?

When you start a business, you hope that it will magically all fall into place, clients will come rushing to you with ease and it will all just work. Whilst that can happen, it's not been my story. That is until I started to do the inner work on me. By the way, that inner work also really helped with my relationship with my son and changed other parts of my life for the better.

When I started out, I knew what I wanted to do. I wanted to help families who, like my own, were struggling. There wasn't much help available, at least not in the Connective Parenting approach I teach. It was relatively new within the UK and there were few opportunities to learn about it. I felt hugely passionate about it as it had had such a big impact on our family for the better, it made me determined to share it with others.

I started a Facebook page and then a group. I shared information and ideas – nothing fancy. I created my own logo with the help of my brother, learnt how to use Canva and off I went. Over time I learnt what worked and what didn't. The group grew gradually to start with, I wasn't good at promoting it but then it got some traction and is now a thriving, supportive, non-judgemental community of people all wanting to support each other and learn. I absolutely love it.

I keep it quite personal, rather than professional, in tone. I wanted, and still do want, to be approachable. I share hope and keep it free of judgement. There's enough judgement out there!

The first few courses I ran in person weren't sold out, but I had enough and got great feedback from them. It felt good and I knew I was doing the right thing, I just needed to keep going and hopefully the business would grow.

It also felt like an uphill battle to get myself known. My confidence wasn't high (despite how it might have appeared) and I would hold myself back, believing I wasn't good enough or qualified enough. All things I sometimes still believe today but now I have enough feedback that I can push that thought away knowing it's not true. I've also done the inner work that helps me when those feelings hit.

I wanted to reach more families and so decided to run courses online (this was a long time before Covid when being online became the norm). I was a leader in running this type of course online and my first course sold out. In fact, I put on another straight away due to the interest. It showed me there was a market and enough parents wanted to learn and find out more. We had parents from all over the country join us, many of whom I'm still in contact with today.

Growing the business was slow through the first few years

and it felt like an uphill battle. I got so annoyed with myself that it wasn't growing more, that I couldn't get to where I wanted to get to. I would see people online apparently doing very well in their much newer businesses and felt like I was failing. I couldn't work out what I was doing wrong. All the strategy I learnt was great, but I didn't have the self-belief to implement it. I was doing the courses, but it wasn't growing the business.

I then started working on me and that was when things really started to change. I worked on my internal belief system using the emotional freedom technique (EFT), hypnotherapy and coaching. It wasn't always easy, but it was worth it. The business started to grow more quickly and I could see the wood for the trees. The downside was I took on too much work sometimes, to the detriment of my family life. There was that voice in my head saying 'it might all disappear so do it now'. That was another belief to work on, although it's still there sometimes it's nowhere near as strong. I changed how I was working slightly so I could help more families, by offering group courses and training, as well as individual sessions.

Then a few months before Covid hit I started working with a coach on me again. I had some huge shifts from this work and it was literally a game changer for my business. The first year of Covid wasn't easy (in fact the second wasn't either), trying to navigate home schooling (we lasted half a day!) and keeping the business afloat so I had an income let alone everything else we all had to cope with. It was however the biggest year I've ever had in my business. At the start I thought I'd lose everything, then I sat down with my coach, came up with a game plan and went for it. I stepped out of my comfort zone realising I had nothing to lose. And it paid off.

Since the start of Covid my business has gone from strength to strength. I've built stronger relationships with the organisations I partner with, we've worked together to think about how we can best help families, and I've built an amazing team.

What lessons have I learnt?

- Balancing work and home isn't easy, especially when you start out in business, but with effort it is doable.
- Do what you love, then it doesn't always feel like work.
- Make sure you take proper time off, ideally weekly, to recharge – burnout is real and hard to recover from.
- Be aligned with your values.
- Do the inner work so you can be you and achieve your potential.
- Surround yourself with people who believe in you and support you.

Where am I going?

As we move away from a personal brand to a company brand, my vision for the business remains the same: to keep working with parents, helping them to create strong connections with their children, understand their needs and create a better, happier world full of understanding and love. I also want to ensure that we continue to offer affordable support alongside our free resources. This is dear to my heart and something I feel is very important, particularly in today's world.

In conclusion

Be prepared! Starting a business…
Takes longer than you think
Costs more than you think
You can't do it all

Whatever you want to do in the world, believe in yourself, do something you're passionate about, make sure it's aligned with your values and you'll fly. The world needs women like us to create a happier world.

So persevere, *it's worth every second of the effort.*

BIO:

Sarah is a single adoptive mum, passionate about helping families.

The team at Connective Family work with families who are struggling with their child's behaviour. They help create a strong connection and reduce the challenges. As part of this work they also train other professionals in their approach.

Sarah is also the author of two books. 'Adopting Solo' shares the first two years of her life as a parent and her second 'Connective Parenting' shares the NVR approach in a simple-to-read guide and is recommended by professionals working with families.

www.connectivefamily.co.uk

23
WANT TO KNOW THE 3 KEYS TO HAPPINESS, SATISFACTION AND SUCCESS?

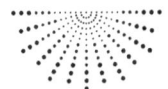

Kim Woods

You know those moments when time stops?

You remember them forever as they indelibly ink themselves into your psyche as the import to your life is so profound, your life changes irrevocably.

I have quite a few about my career tattooed in my brain.

It's circa 1995 and I'm standing in the CEO's office asking for support for another ridiculous deadline that's absolutely impossible to achieve. It's end of day on a Friday and my boss, the CFO, has asked me for an 80-hour job to be completed by Sunday morning.

"You told me to come to you if I ever needed anything," I state hopefully as he's given me his full attention.

"Yes?"

"That's why I'm here," I continue, "Is there anything you can do for us?"

"Like what?"

That's the thing. The only way to help the situation is for the CEO to give the CFO a directive or to go to other C-level executives and direct them to help us.

"Would you talk to Arthur (the CFO) to relax the deadline?"

He shakes his head.

"Would you get us more support? You can ask internally as we've pitched in for other teams a number of times. We could really use the help right now."

He grimaces.

"Well…" he says.

I lose track of all of the reasons he states about how this isn't an appropriate ask and how my team should basically just suck it up.

I walk out of his office, knowing I'm not as valuable to the company as most of the other directors.

That's it – the bottom line.

I. AM. NOT. AS. VALUABLE.

The truth stares me in the face as he wouldn't even make the effort to ask for help on my behalf.

I practically collapse on the floor. I'm reeling…after all the hours, foregoing weekends, vacations, basically putting my life on hold, for what?

I pick myself up and of course, find another job – where, you guessed it, it's more of the same, but I don't know that yet.

Here are a few highlights:

I wrangle a lost client from the edge and pull out all the stops to make an impossible situation possible only to find myself in the boardroom with the client and my team as he kicks everyone out.

He proceeds to loom over me, yelling at the top of his lungs, "You think you know so much little girl. I don't take advice from little girls who don't know anything. I've been here much longer than you've been alive."

He turns beet red and screams for another 10 minutes.

I've lost track of what he's saying as I'm trying to figure out how to save the client engagement.

Yes, not a single thought goes through my head about how inappropriate this is, how viciously I'm being treated or how I should stand up and walk away.

I'm thinking about saving the client engagement.

This type of thing happens over and over again.

A CFO in Boston actually stands up and pounds his hands on the table demonstrating how mad he is until he sits back down in his chair and laughs at how he's not yelling at me. He's yelling to let off steam and informs me that I'm one of the best people he's ever worked with, so I would never have to experience that spectacle.

Oh, but didn't I just experience it?

Fast forward a few years and a new position later and the client CEO is the one yelling – screaming actually.

I'm supposed to be selecting my wedding rings with my soon-to-be husband, but instead I'm standing in for the partner of our firm at 7:00 pm on a weekend evening.

The CEO is turning purple.

He's screaming about the $5M engagement and how it's going off the rails. It's all my fault. Why haven't I prevented this? What am I doing to make sure it gets back on track? Why am I just sitting there, shouldn't I be doing something?

What actually? I have no authority to do anything about this client engagement. I'm merely heading one small piece of it.

I separate myself from this situation and think, I need a new job.

Of course, I find one in a hot minute and continue to get myself into the same situation over and over again.

My father's in the hospital with a critical condition and I've told my boss I need to take a few hours off to go see him. My boss whines for an hour about how hard it'll be for him without me to…basically, do his job.

After being in 4 states during the week, I return to my apartment at 9 pm on a Thursday evening, only to get a call about a critical deal that needs to be closed at 8 am the next morning in New Jersey. Instead of taking a much-needed break, I'm heading out to save another deal. *(This happens every week for way too long.)*

I'm flying, way too late in my pregnancy, to close a deal *(and of course, do)* when the flight attendant expresses more concern for my unborn child than anyone at my company.

This is the pattern. I save everyone, put them first and make everyone's life better. I solve their problems, listen to their lunacy and close their deals. When I leave, they hire 3 people to do the work I've done all by myself. I make millions of dollars for any company in which I work.

AND.

What am I doing for ME? Am I valuing myself? Am I putting my needs first? Do I even know what my needs are?

I'm working too hard and taking too much grief to live this way throughout my entire career.

I want to be successful, but I also want to be satisfied. I want to be valued. Respected. Appreciated.

There must be a different way. I've been doing it all wrong for too many years to count. How can I change this? I have no idea.

I'm smart. I work hard. I have amazing skills. But nothing's working. What's wrong?

How can I be doing so much and not be valued? How can I be so successful and not happy? How can I be reaching so far and not be fulfilled?

Does this sound familiar? Can you relate to putting EVERYONE else's needs, wants and desires first?

It takes me too long to recognize I'm not doing anything right.

In fact, I'm doing everything exactly wrong.

It takes me over a decade-and-a-half to get to the truth. It takes my son being born with significant developmental issues and my pursuit of everything ancient wisdom and modern practical methods. It takes my husband almost dying and me having to pursue even more eastern techniques. It takes everything and more. YET.

I **finally** figure it out. I need to go inward for the answers. I need to be silent and listen to my **intuition**. I need to follow my intuition again and again until I **trust it**.

What have I been doing wrong?

Every. Single Thing.

I've been looking outside of myself. I've been defining myself by other's definition of success. I've been reaching, striving and not meeting my own needs – ever.

Sound familiar?

I hear you. I see you. I know you.

I've been there – for too damn long.

For those of you caught in the throes of your mind and being swallowed up by triggers, I see you.

For those of you not reaching for support and opportunity to get you toward your own goals, I'm here for you.

For those who can see the potential of your best life but are too afraid to jump, I know you.

I'm anchoring your full potential until you can realize it for yourself.

Why?

I've lived it. I've been caught in all of the thorns. I've trapped myself up again and again. I've struggled to get out.

I'm passionate about this not happening to anyone else.

It isn't until I allow my intuition to take the lead in making decisions and directing my life, do I change my ways.

It isn't until I like myself enough to stand in my power to say enough is enough long before an angry person is looming over me yelling at the top of his lungs.

It isn't until I trust myself enough to follow my own definition of success to be fulfilled, happy and satisfied.

However, it takes too much from me.

It takes me being screamed at all over the country by angry men.

It takes my son being born with significant development issues.

It takes my husband almost dying.

It takes just too damn much.

Now.

I can't allow this to happen to anyone else.

In fact, I'm rabid about this not happening to anyone else.

I will not let anyone get caught up by other's needs, wants and desires, to be thrown off their own course by other's greed or manipulations.

I will not have the acceptable and conforming approach of societal norms or familial expectations override the unique success path of each and every person.

I'll not have a single person within my sphere unable to realize their full potential as well as their birthright of purpose, power and prosperity.

I'm beyond compelled to show you the way - to help you live your own definition of success, have strong relationships and attract as much love and money you desire.

I. AM. HERE. FOR. YOU.

I see you. I hear you. I know you.

How do I separate you from the needs and expectations of others to live your best life; one filled with satisfaction, respect and success?

I've created my revolutionary Do You Know, Like and Trust Yourself™ method that weaves the magic of the intuitive world with the practicalities of business and life.

Because when you follow my method to know, like and trust yourself fully, you:

- Make decisions based on *your own definition of success*
- Understand what *satisfies* and *fulfills* you
- *Stand in your power* to eliminate people taking advantage of you
- Smoothly attract *support* and *opportunity*
- Have more *passion* and *energy*
- Easily able to *successfully grow* your business
- Draw *more love* and *money* into your life
- Connect beautifully with your *soul mate clients*
- Make your *dreams* come true

This is my passion.

When you follow my True Know-Like-Trust Method™, you're able to fulfill your success desires without giving up pieces of yourself. You become so much MORE of you.

Do you feel satisfied with your success, enjoy your relationships and draw love and money into your life?

Or have you been reading with excitement of what's possible for you?

Don't settle in your life, even if it's fraught with reasons or things holding you back.

This is your life – right here and right now.

Live it to the fullest.

BIO:

Kim Woods, The Intuitive Business Strategist, teaches high-performing entrepreneurs to Know, Like and Trust themselves, creating radical levels of satisfaction in every aspect of their lives.

Kim's a highly sought after business leader with countless master-level intuitive certifications paired with 25+ years of C-suite business experience. She's led 425+ business leaders, overseen $65M+ in sales and influenced 300,000+ team members. Kim has an incredibly solid depth of field for combining business with intuition, creating shockingly transformative results. Her clients range from Fortune 500 companies & $MM CEO's to solopreneurs and creatives.

Kim has been featured in Yahoo, Forbes, INC, Entrepreneur, ABC, CBS, NBC, USA Today, Reader's Digest, Fox News, Market Watch and Digital Journal.

www.kimwoods.com

24
DO IT BEFORE YOU'RE READY!

Jill Chitty

P icture this: I stood at the side of the stage in my underwear...
5 - 4 – 3 -
The Stage Manager counted down my entrance.
The Wardrobe Lady quickly wrapped my skirt around my waist...
2 -
Another slipped on a shirt...
1 -
And handed me my scarf.
GO!
I walked onto the back of the stage in my chorus line - my blouse undone, my scarf in my hand.
3 seconds later I was at the foot of the stage in front of a packed house...
Ready to sing my line and deliver my words.

Fully dressed, professional, calm and smiling.

No one ever knew... but the director saw and was impressed...

I was 12.

I've needed to call on that calm resilience many times since as I navigated growing my business.

To the outsider it may look as if it all came easily, like I had it all together... I know differently!

This has been the pattern for my business over the years, start before I'm ready and turn up with a smile.

So, if you're feeling crap right now, overwhelmed, even ashamed of where you still find yourself, read on...

That experience set a flame in my heart to perform more, so after leaving school I earned myself a few years' experience in the world before going to drama school... it was all I ever wanted to do.

I had no idea how hugely entrepreneurial acting was, researching, learning and delivering over and over again. Marketing myself and building relationships was something I naturally did every time I went for a new role.

A large dose of resilience was needed to keep going with castings and auditions and rejection after rejection.

Fast forward 3 years and I was out in the big world getting a few acting jobs then waitressing.

Going on a UK tour then doing bar work and living in this cycle of working and waiting.

It was hard.

And I was poor!

Eventually, I got married and we moved to Gibraltar where an opportunity opened up to work for the BBC and have my own TV show. I loved the small crew I worked with each week and the amazing people I had the privilege of interviewing.

Sadly, the time came to move back to the UK as we were

starting a family, so I waved goodbye to the TV show and headed back home.

Son number one was born and all I can say is 'WOW! That hurt!'.

I had decided that it wasn't tenable to be an actress anymore [or my husband did!] as theatre work had turned to touring and with a young family it was tough to leave them for long periods.

However, a move down south opened up a TV opportunity once again as I began working very part time with Granada TV on a lunchtime magazine show.

My second son was born.

All was looking great!

Until an anonymous phone call told me my husband was having an affair.

At 32 I lost it all.

Marriage. Job. Home.

I found myself moving back into my mum's house with a 4 and 1 year old with nothing to show for my 32 years but a few clothes and my 2 gorgeous sons.

I was broken

But I was entrepreneurial...

And this is where my business journey began.

I'd like to say I started a business because I wanted to serve people or add value... I didn't!

I wanted to earn money on my terms and have the freedom to be there for my boys as I solo-parented them.

The next few years were tough. I discovered I had been married to a narcissist and needed time to gather myself from the unravelling I had experienced.

A chance conversation with my brother about my future sparked an idea in my head... that was all it took.

That night I planned a whole business; model, name and strategy and over the next few weeks pulled everything together.

It was a makeover party business for girls and we were Glitter & Gloss!

I literally cajoled three friends into coming onboard [one who had only just had a baby] and together we launched and took my county by storm.

It was crazy fun but after a year my friends moved on to other projects and I chose to run and develop the business on my own.

Courtesy of the government, I was given a business coach and she said when she talked to me about my business it was like she was speaking a foreign language to me… she was right!

I had a long way to go…

From that time on I spent endless nights after putting the kids to sleep at my bedroom desk trying to work out what on earth marketing was and how we could grow and improve our offering.

Slowly, the business started to form and I sold it as an award-winning business with 17 staff 12 years later.

It was my baby, where I cut my teeth on marketing and learned to lead a team. But I had worked almost endlessly for those 12 years every week and weekend – I was exhausted.

I had been headhunted by a top UK entrepreneur to run a local team and began a very different kind of adventure.

This was my first foray into B2B marketing.

By this stage my kids were teenagers and for anyone who has been a parent of teenagers you'll understand it's a roller-coaster ride! Managing my business at the same time was often extremely difficult and my self-care plunged to non-existent.

During one team meeting we were all asked how many leads we had won on LinkedIn?

Linked what?

Never heard of it!

A quick whisper to a colleague gave me the promise of the low down later.

Isn't it funny how life dips and bends and takes us around corners we could never have imagined navigating around?

Social media was still in its early stages and not having grown up with it, it didn't come naturally.

I immediately created a profile, connected with anyone willing and messaged them everyday to join my weekly workshop, and yes... that's called spamming. [I didn't know any better!]

Instantly, I was thrown off LinkedIn.

Not wanting to lose face with my team I begged my way back on and decided it was time to learn properly.

I re-thought my profile, how I reached out to my network and within two weeks won two contracts worth £21K.

That was 11 years ago. I've been a LinkedIn consultant since.

It seemed to come naturally to me, but as I look back I can see how my disparate and varied history came into play in a unique way.

Permit me to run through some of those with you around LinkedIn:

The Profile:

The temptation here is to write about yourself, your journey and what you're great at. But LinkedIn is an enormous introduction platform and no-one cares about you... yet!

The secret is building trust by showing you understand their world and have the means and understanding to get them from A to B in a reasonable timeframe.

The directors who auditioned me weren't interested in my experience so much as, could they bet on me to deliver the role... they had to see that character in me, so couldn't make it all about Jill.

Connecting:

As LinkedIn has developed, my approach has definitely shifted. Behind each profile is a real person and we need to reach out accordingly. Spending time researching a person before connecting or commenting if they had posted recently gave context to that.

When I was acting there was no such thing as social media – it was the library – LOL! But it became a key piece for me to research not only the role I was up for, but the director and theatre company too… it gave weight to my presence and sometimes was the thing that tipped favour my way. It built relationships.

Content:

Writing content on LinkedIn is a crucial way to stay top of mind, build your authority and have some great conversations. As we developed my TV show it became apparent there were two agendas; what we wanted to talk about and what our audience wanted to hear. Our viewing stats soared when we shared what interested our audience.

Content for me on LinkedIn became less of showcasing 'Jill' but more of what information would my future clients need to know about me, my programmes, results, processes and values etc.

Systems:

For years I baulked against systemising my LinkedIn marketing and yet it was the systems that made Glitter & Gloss so successful.

We had marketing systems, onboarding systems, processes for a successful party and follow up systems and so on.

So ever so slowly I began creating connecting systems,

systems for messaging, systems for following up with engagers and it made life on LinkedIn much more efficient, clear and enjoyable.

Giving:

Throughout my time as a business owner I have had multiple people generously sow into me and my business. It's meant the world to me and made all the difference.

It took me a while to realise this principle needs to play out on LinkedIn too. Each week you'll find me answering questions in my inbox, jumping onto calls to explain or doing a Loom video for extra clarity – my way of giving back. We've also translated that into our content strategy and each week we have a useful giveaway people can download and they do in their hundreds!

This has led to connections messaging me saying. 'I'm so glad I found you,' and 'I'm your new number one fan!'. It's so easy to give value and my mantra is 'Give away your best stuff as no one ever grew a successful business giving away their worst.'.

Converting:

As I get older I can look back over the years and see how I have overcome the trauma in my childhood and in my marriage to find a better me, but money was always elusive. I was constantly living on an extremely tight budget and often overusing my credit cards.

Converting leads into sales was something I was anxious about and certainly obsessed with and I'm sure people will have sensed that.

What started to emerge was all the above began to work in my favour and took the pressure off making sales.

I finally learned to sit back and enjoy the process and focus on building relationships.

I learned to trust myself and God more that the right clients would come in.

Running a business isn't linear – like you do something once and get it right the first time... no!

It's trial and error.

Putting it out there and improving it.

I wasn't wrong as I fumbled my way through lack of growth, massive mistakes, creating programmes nobody signed up for, spending hours working without clarity... It's all part of the beautiful mix of running your own business.

There was no map for my exact journey and there will be no map for your specific journey because you get to create it.

And therein lies both the struggle and the joy.

If I had one thing to say to younger Jill it would be 'forgive yourself and be kind to you'.

Enjoy the adventure!

BIO:

People Empowerer, Business Builder and Community Creator. Jill works with solopreneurs right through to global brands consulting and training on how LinkedIn can be ***the*** marketing tool that tips the scales towards massive growth.

She takes the pressure off Coaches and Consultants with her systems and integration with LinkedIn and other platforms.

Jill and her team also manage LinkedIn accounts and create content strategies so businesses always have a strong presence.

Her passion is sharing with those in business who've experienced trauma.

www.linkedin.com/in/jillchitty-linked-inmarketing

25
MY JOURNEY TO TODAY

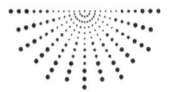

Elyse Burns-Hill

I have always been passionate about business, possibly because I've come from a line of entrepreneurial thinkers beginning with at least my grandfather, who started out importing wine and was on the bleeding edge of importing bottled water (way before it was trendy). He ran several other businesses over the years before sadly passing away from a sudden brain aneurysm at 56. My parents also ran businesses, so I grew up listening to 'business owner conversations' from when I was very young. All my entrepreneurial family members experienced some business successes and had some opportunities to learn from things that hadn't panned out entirely as they'd intended.

When I was 15, I started teaching myself HTML – the primary coding language of websites. Then I learnt PHP – a more dynamic coding language. With that knowledge and experience I was building up, I started building websites for other people. That first business experience was exhilarating, and I wanted to do more. So, I started exploring this brand-new internet marketing world that was beginning to take off. My Mum was a Marketing Consultant, so I already had a base level of understanding of marketing from listening to her talk (it's incredible how much I've learnt from my Mum over the years, simply from listening to her speak to others!).

I dabbled in business and marketing over the next few years while I finished school and then studied zoology at university. You might wonder 'why on earth zoology?' when I've just talked about how much I enjoyed business. At that point, I still hadn't considered anything business related as a career. It was my hobby! I look back and think how ridiculous that sounds, that I enjoyed something and never pursued it or even considered it something I wanted to create my future life around.

Over the next few years, I jumped around jobs working for my parent's business and in sales roles in the Apple Premium Reseller stores in Guernsey and a few years later in Jersey. I considered joining the Royal Navy as a helicopter pilot – ok, I didn't consider; I went most of the way through the application process and was told I'd be better suited to the Observer role (apparently, I'd smashed it in the aptitude testing, while I wasn't so strong on the pilot score). The Observer is the person in control of the navigation and weapons systems up in the helicopter, and it was the control over the weapons system that I couldn't get my head around – the risk of unintended victims when I pressed the button. So there ended my ambitions of joining the Royal Navy!

It wasn't until I was 24 and living in Malta that I decided that I wanted to study for my accountancy qualification. My Dad has always said I should be an accountant because he thought I'd be great at it. I'd always poo-pooed the idea because I didn't want a boring job in a boring office sitting behind a boring desk – joining the Royal Navy seemed like a much better idea! Until one day, I sat on the balcony of our apartment in Malta, sipping a cup of tea (well, I am English even if I was in a Mediterranean country!), and my mind was quiet enough to hear my voice of intuition: *"train to be an accountant"*.

Accountancy would give me a fantastic foundation in finance which is one of the essential things in business – why do we run a business? To make a profit. You don't have a business if you don't make a profit. So, finance and money underpin all of that. Add the financial training to the websites, marketing, and sales experience I'd gained over the previous few years; I'd be amazingly placed to "do business" in the future (whatever "doing business" meant).

I started studying for my ACCA qualification at home on my own, did the first two exams completely unsupported and passed them. Then I got accepted onto the training programme at PwC Malta, where I studied for and passed the next couple of exams (including the Maltese variant of the Business Law exam, where I had to learn the Maltese case law names…in Maltese!). My next jump was moving to Jersey and into a smaller midsize firm, where I stayed for over three years.

In 2015, I moved back to the UK with my partner, Patrick, with whom I have since had my two gorgeous daughters. That is when I decided to give my business ideas a go, I picked up a couple of clients, but I wasn't committed to what I was doing. Looking back, I believe I wasn't getting anywhere because I didn't have a vision or a belief in myself. I still had some more growing to do. So, when my eldest was three months old, Patrick handed in his notice at his job to stay home and look after the baby, and I went back into full-time employment at a local accountancy firm.

For 18 months, I plugged away at learning and acquiring more knowledge and understanding – on a technical level on how to do my job, but also on a personal level – watching how the client managers and Directors did their jobs so that I could learn what they do. Then my mind and body hit a metaphorical brick wall. I returned to full-time work when my first baby was three months old. That meant that my body was only three months recovered after delivering a baby for the first time, which had also involved surgery and a blood transfusion. Becoming a parent for the first time is also a new adventure that takes some mental and emotional adjustment. In retrospect, I'm not convinced I was ready to tackle a stressful work environment full-time just three months after birth. The Mum guilt I felt leaving my daughter at home every morning was horrendous, and I don't think that ever subsided for the full 18 months I was working full time. Oh, and I was still producing and pumping milk for the first six months, after which I couldn't keep putting my body through it! So really, it's no surprise I crashed after 18 months – it's amazing I kept going for as long as I did!

I took time to get myself sorted out and back to a good place physically and mentally. I worked on being a good Mummy, being good to myself, and of course, working on little side projects because I'm incapable of not thinking about business-related topics for more than 5 minutes. At one seminar I attended, run by a local Action Coach, I met another accountant – we were the only two accountants in the room. We had a quick chat at the end of the seminar, and he had to rush off for a client meeting but asked if I would meet with him again soon. My intuitive voice spoke to me again and said I needed to talk to this guy; it was connected to my bigger picture. I agreed and gave him my phone number, and a week later, we sat drinking tea and talking.

Craig ran a local accountancy firm with a small team, one of whom was just about to go off on maternity leave, so he asked if I'd be willing to do a bit of subcontracting for him to help with the workload while his team member was off. He was also starting to pick up clients who were using Xero, and as none of his team had much experience with Xero, and as I was marketing myself as a Xero specialist, there was a connection too good to miss. It suited both of us, I didn't want to be taking on too much work (as I was still recovering from my last bout of over-work!), and he needed someone for sporadic jobs and occasional support with deadlines.

Life was going well, and we decided to add our second daughter to our family. I continued working part-time and managed everything reasonably well with a baby bouncing on my lap. That's when things started to change. Craig was diagnosed with cancer and, in April 2020, appointed me associate director of his accountancy firm and asked me to get my accountancy practising certificate sorted out with my professional body so that he could make me a full director. He'd been given the bad news that his cancer was terminal, so he asked me to take over the firm and look after all our clients. Sadly, his health deteriorated faster than I was able to get my practising certificate through ACCA, my professional body. I decided to drop my Chartered membership and join the Institute of Financial Accounting to get my practising certificate more quickly. They were fabulous and sorted me out within five weeks, and on 1st October 2020, I became a full director. Twenty-six days later, Craig passed away.

I learned a tremendous amount from Craig while we were working together. In my mind, we'd be working together for years to come – we balanced each other with skills and personality (albeit his technical skills and experience were many years more than mine!). It was a heart-wrenching loss for me to lose him while I felt we still had so much to accomplish together. I embraced his request to continue to look after all our clients with every fibre of my being.

For a long time, I had an uncomfortable mix of emotions to deal with:

- Grief at losing Craig from my life so early, he was only 48, and he should have had years more to leave his mark on the world and the lives and businesses of our clients.
- Excitement at having my own 'real' business to work with, finally having the opportunity to put all my experience into practice.
- Guilt at feeling excited because none of this would have happened if it hadn't been for Craig's death. It took me a long time to get my head around this one.

I've been on a massive learning curve since taking over the firm, and I've realised that it is a place I thrive because one of my core strengths is a love of learning. It's been hard work. *Really* hard work. If I thought it was hard work studying for professional level exams while working full time, that was easy compared to the last nearly two years since I took over. I've had my moments of struggling physically, mentally and emotionally because I had stopped listening to my intuition and wasn't treating my mind or body with enough respect to give it the care, rest and nourishment it needed.

I'm still pushing new boundaries (while respecting the essential self-care boundaries!) and constantly learning new things. As I write this, I'm exploring a merger with another firm, which is a new experience and learning curve.

If I had to give one piece of advice to anyone in business, that would be to get a mentor, coach or therapist or even a peer group to meet with regularly to talk about yourself, how YOU are coping with life and business and family and everything else you're looking after. A safe place to offload your concerns and worries and get an external viewpoint on what's happening. It's the best investment I've ever made and essential for keeping yourself well.

BIO:

Elyse Burns-Hill is an accountant and business advisor. She runs two accountancy firms, each specialising in different business sectors. She has written Amazon best-selling books and created the "PARSAQ Bookkeeping Method", which helps small business owners do their own bookkeeping in an efficient and stress-free way – watch out for the book – it will be published by the end of 2022! Her aim in business is to help people scale up their businesses to live their best lives. Ultimately, the big picture in life is to help reduce stress and anxiety in the lives of entrepreneurs, business owners and self-employed people.

www.elyseburns-hill.com

26
A RISING MIND, LIKE A RISING TIDE, LIFTS ALL BOATS

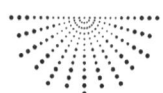

Harry Mansfield

A feeling, a thought and then action – the process of starting any business. Whether the idea for your business is, or was, a light bulb moment, or a slow burner, the reality of running a legitimate and successful business is totally different from the initial excitement. To fulfil your business goal you need a very strong mind.

Understanding how your own mind works, and knowing how to use it to your advantage, is paramount in getting your business to succeed. Just think how much more productive you are when you jump out of bed in the morning rather than when you don't want to get up! You do not have to invest in expensive equipment, or facilities, you are making full use of a very powerful tool that you already have. A great business strategy! When using your mind in the right way you will accomplish what you want for your business, whatever your chosen industry, whilst at the same time looking after yourself.

There is a long list of stages that are needed to be put into place when starting and running a business. Each of you will prioritise them differently but with all of them you will need to put in a lot of effort. From researching your competitors, financing the business, understanding the legal aspects of your industry, hiring help and, getting realistic about the risk involved, your mind is the foundation of being and staying strong throughout all of these developments.

I started my business in 2018 and it seems like a lifetime ago! Along the way I have had several major set-backs, all of which have been completely beyond my control, but I don't regret my decision for a moment. I have a strong mind because I use the MindPower Proficiency® skills that I teach and so, despite the set-backs, the business is still working! In 2019 my expected business partner changed the agreed business share from a straight 50/50 percent split to 75/25 percent in their favour. Understandably I stopped working with them and modified the business structure accordingly which took a good deal of time. In 2020, like many other businesses, I had to close due to lockdown and I didn't come under any government scheme to help me financially to sustain the business. Since beginning my business I have been going through a difficult divorce where in 2021 my ex-husband's behaviour jeopardised how and where I run my business.

Having experienced these additional struggles to the normal stresses of running a business I know that by using my mind in the right way has been the secret to getting through all these challenges. For this reason I would like to share with you the MindPower Proficiency® foundation techniques for your business, and for you, to benefit from.

Firstly, understanding how your mind works is essential. Controlling your mind will help you succeed in the running of your business. Your mind controls your brain and body so, when you are looking for positivity to lead a team, clarity and focus in a business task, an increase in productivity, and strength when the challenges of balancing your personal life arise, you will be successful.

ETA is a technique which allows you to understand how your mind works when you are at work. It stops your mind from being distracted from other factors in your life and spiralling in the wrong direction due to business challenges.

EMOTION: In these recent years of pandemics and lockdowns the acceptance of a persons' emotions has increased but little has been done to know how best to deal with it. It is the feeling you feel and it is what it is. You and your team will experience totally different feelings from the same situation at work. By recognising your emotion, either positive or challenging, you will have the information needed to move forwards in the best way for the project you are working on.

THOUGHT: This is where you and your team need to learn what to change. The mind naturally magnifies your emotion unless it is trained not to, for example, worried about feeling anxious, or pleased about being happy. A trained mind will stop this in its tracks so you are simply aware of the emotion and are able to accept it. You will work more effectively and be constructive at work.

ACTION: If the thought is correct your actions at work will be fruitful. When trained, your mind can stop in its tracks the natural process of working in a subconscious way, reducing your awareness, rather than a conscious way, which will produce the correct action wanted for your business assignment.

To get your mind, and your team's mind fitter for the workplace, the following four MindPower Proficiency® techniques will help you be mentally strong so you can unleash your best business mind. When put into practice you will have the foundation for strong mental health for the business world.

Your brain is changeable so you can alter your Neuronal

Pathways. For a successful business the following Foundation Four Mindpower Proficiency® techniques will enlighten you to your habits, and teach you how to manage and alter your behaviour. You will be a more confident you in your place of work and able to manage eventualities in a much calmer and stronger way.

Your mind is an incredibly powerful tool but becoming mentally strong doesn't happen overnight. A professional sportsman repeats his, or her, moves over and over and over again so that they become streamlined and successful. Here is the start of that process for you, your mind and your business.

Mental Health Check In

Our mind is changing continuously and at great speed. You must become aware of your mind throughout each day to become mentally strong for your business. Knowing what your mind is doing is the starting point for you to train and raise your mind. This baseline reference allows you to become mentally aware and more powerful in business.

Choose a time of day which works for you to do a *Mental Health Check-In*. Think about what you are feeling and thinking at that moment in time. No doubt you have a busy schedule, so do it at the same time you do things that are automatic to you, for example when you're turning your computer on or, making a drink!

Like anything in life, practice will make it more automatic and recognising your baseline at that moment in time will become easily identifiable. Once recognised, you then must put it into place over and over again throughout your day. If you are not aware of how you feel at a moment in time you can't do anything positive about it – either to keep yourself calm and level-headed or, to really relish and enjoy the positives of your work.

Mindpower Scale

We use the *Mindpower Scale* after establishing your baseline from your *Mental Health Check-In* to enable you to put into place the right action. The *MindPower Scale* is comparable to an MRI of your mind; giving you the information to raise and strengthen your mind for your industry!

Below is the scale you are working from:

Positive 1 - 5
Positive 6 - 10
Challenge 1 - 5
Challenge 6 - 10

Positive lower numbers, 1-5, eg feeling of calm and composed

Challenging lower numbers, 1-5, eg feeling of sadness and feeling low

Positive higher numbers, 6–10, eg feeling of happiness and excitement

Challenging higher number, 6-10, eg feeling of anxiousness and worry

If you know where you are on the *Mindpower Scale*, whether you land on the positive side of the scale or the challenging one, you can choose what technique is best for you to put into place to get mentally strong or, maintain your mental strength for whatever business situation you find yourself in.

You are now Mentally Aware. From this you are able to start training your mind to work in your favour at work.

Challenge Not Negative

This technique shows the importance of phrasing and clean language. We listen to what we say to ourselves and you need to say the correct words and terminology to train your mind. This skill also works really well when performing with others around you; your team and your clients.

Start by calling a negative a *Challenge*, this gets your mind thinking in a more positive way which slows down and stops any natural negative thinking patterns which you have in the subconscious part of your mind. Your mind naturally remembers the past, so difficult times in your life will come to the fore unless you train it not to.

Crucially, when training your mind this way there is a solution to a *challenge* whereas there isn't with a negative, it is just a dead end and in business, we always need a solution! When running a business you have to continuously be looking forward and phrasing your *challenges* correctly as it is vital to gain the best solution for you to move forward.

Three Positives to One Challenge

Whatever your numbers are on the *Mindpower Scale* and whichever group; positive or challenging, the first thing to do is to attain the positives. The mind believes what you tell it so feed it positives.

Training and teaching your mind to be strong, like any other part of your body, needs guidance and repetition. It automatically focuses on the negatives, which as I said before are actually challenges, so, for every one of your challenges it has to be balanced off with *three positives*.

It does not matter how small your positives are, it is just a case of always making sure that your challenge is outweighed with *three positives* to keep training your mind to rise up and become mentally stronger. When I worked as a sports coach this technique changed the mind of my clients and as such their actions. Throughout a working day challenges will appear, but your mind can be in a state which embraces and focuses on the positives, however small, and you can really appreciate them, celebrate them and build on them to get you working more efficiently.

Your stronger mind will make you happier, you will be more productive and you will feel physically better. This positive outlook will make you more focused and efficient in your work.

Looking for those *three positives* when faced with your business challenges is an important mantra to have when facing them.

Conclusion

By putting these initial four techniques into practice, we are:

- Training our mind to become aware of the emotions that we are feeling
- We are not allowing our mind to escalate and spiral
- We can act with a conscious mind to decide what is the appropriate action

It is from this foundation that you can use your mind to move forwards with resilience and be more productive in your business. When you learn this, you become a master of your own mind, troubling thoughts about your business will come and go like white clouds moving across a clear blue sky.

The *MindPower Proficiency® Foundation Four* is part of my registered behaviour model, *The Transformation Triangle®*, to train the mind. Firstly, be *Aware* of what your mind is doing when at work and how it reacts, then *Challenge* your mind, along with your teams, to put the correct procedure in place. You can *Transform* your mind so you can **ACT** in a way that works for you and your business to succeed.

Being under pressure is part of life, particularly in business, and it is essential for you to use your mind for success. If you raise your mind it will brighten the path for your business and colleagues around you in any given situation.

. . .

BIO:

Harry Mansfield, known as "The MindPower Champion", teaches the profitable skills of using the mind to streamline businesses.

She realised how powerful the mind is when training to parachute and when working as a sports coach. Her CPD registered centre trains for performance in industry.

www.linktr.ee/harrymansfield

ABOUT THE DAISY CHAIN GROUP

Trudy Simmons started The Daisy Chain Group in 2010. It was started to support and encourage businesswomen to have a safe space to share their journeys, to grow their businesses and to be seen and heard in their endeavours.

Since its inception, the concept has grown to include platforms for women to find their voice and become more visible in lots of different ways. Whether it is attending online networking events, committing to co-working time together, learning from experts in masterclasses or investing in monthly business coaching to boost your clarity, direction, focus, accountability and momentum, we all need to find the space to work ON our businesses.

If you have a story to share, come and be a part of the Shine On You Crazy Daisy book series and share your story, or be on the Shine On You Crazy Daisy Podcast to give your story gravitas and hear it in your own voice.

Trudy is known for her engaged communities on Facebook – Businesswomen Shine Online and The Hampshire Women's Business Group

HAVING FUN in your business is a core value of The Daisy

ABOUT THE DAISY CHAIN GROUP

Chain Group. Having fun and TAKING ACTION is what builds you AND your business.

You can find The Daisy Chain Group here:
https://www.thedaisychaingroup.com
https://www.facebook.com/daisychaingroup
https://www.instagram.com/daisychaingroup/
https://www.linkedin.com/in/trudysimmons/

You can find The Daisy Chain Group communities here:
https://www.facebook.com/groups/businesswomenshineonline
https://www.facebook.com/groups/hampshirewomensbusiness

You can find our services here:

Shine On You Crazy Daisy Membership - https://www.thedaisychaingroup.com/shine-on-you-crazy-daisy-membership

You can listen to the Shine On You Crazy Daisy Podcast here:
https://www.thedaisychaingroup.com/podcasts/shine-on-you-crazy-daisy

EVERY TIME YOU BUY FROM A SMALL BUSINESS, THEY DO A HAPPY DANCE!

PLEASE SUPPORT THE BUSINESSES IN THIS BOOK.

CHARITY LINK

10% of the profits from this book will be donated to Healthcare Workers' Foundation Family Fund. The fund will support the children and families of healthcare workers who have passed due to Covid-19. To donate or support this incredible charity, please go to this link – www.healthcareworkersfoundation.org

OTHER BOOKS

SHINE ON YOU CRAZY DAISY BOOK SERIES

AVAILABLE NOW

> **Shine On You Crazy Daisy – Volume 1**
> **Shine On You Crazy Daisy – Volume 2**
> **Shine On You Crazy Daisy – Volume 3**
> **Shine On You Crazy Daisy – Volume 4**
> **Shine On You Crazy Daisy – Volume 5**

Available on Amazon, iBook and in all good bookshops.

www.ingramcontent.com/pod-product-compliance
Lightning Source LLC
Chambersburg PA
CBHW072052110526
44590CB00018B/3138